Series authors:
Malcolm Mann
Steve Taylore-Knowles

Laser A2

Workbook with key

includes material for KET

MACMILLAN

Macmillan Education
Between Towns Road, Oxford OX4 3PP
A division of Macmillan Publishers Limited

Companies and representatives throughout the world

ISBN 978-0-230-42476-0 (with Answer key)
978-0-230-42477-7 (without Answer key)

Series authors: Malcolm Mann & Steve Taylore-Knowles

First published 2012

Original design by Peter Burgess
Page make-up by Peter Burgess
Illustrated by Ilias Arahovitis pp7, 20, 25, 40, 49, 76;
Red Giraffe pp21, 36, 48, 52, 64, 93;
Alek Sotirovski pp17, 19, 27, 65, 85.
Cover design by Peter Burgess
Picture research by Susannah Jayes

The author and publishers would like to thank the following for permission to reproduce their photographs:

Alamy/Greg Balfour Evans p34, Alamy/Incamerastock p11, Alamy/MBI p46, Alamy/Purestock p70, Alamy/Rubberball p9, Alamy/Alex Serge p82, Alamy/SimonHS p44, Alamy/Trevor Smithers ARPS p30, Alamy/Finnbarr Webster p45; **Corbis**/Stephanie Grewel p38, Corbis/ImageSource p57, Corbis/Sean Justice p5; **Getty Images**/Daley and Newton p24, Getty Images/John P. Kelly p80, Getty Images/White Packert p8; **Goodshot** p12; **Imagesource** p31; **Photolibrary**/Photoalto p60; **Topfoto** p69.

Printed and bound by Martins the Printers, Berwick upon Tweed

2016 2015 2014 2013 2012
10 9 8 7 6 5 4 3 2

Contents

1 **The Youth of Today!** page 4
2 **Having Fun!** 10
Check your progress! | Units 1–2 16
3 **Tell me a Story!** 17
4 **Let's Celebrate!** 23
Check your progress! | Units 3–4 29
5 **Off we Go!** 30
6 **Doing it Right!** 36
Check your progress! | Units 5–6 42
7 **Make it, Build it!** 43
8 **Weird World!** 49
Check your progress! | Units 7–8 55
9 **Want any more?** 56
10 **All Sorts of People!** 62
Check your progress! | Units 9–10 68
11 **Looking Good!** 69
12 **It's a Goal!** 75
Check your progress! | Units 11–12 81
13 **Right Time, Right Place!** 82
14 **Words and Pictures!** 88
Check your progress! | Units 13–14 94
Check your progress! | Units 1–14 95
Answer key 96
Audioscripts 107

1

The Youth of Today!

Reading

1 Read the profiles and for each question, choose the correct answer, A, B or C.

I don't wake up very early on school days. I always get up at 7.45am, have a shower, eat breakfast and leave home at 8.30. I know that's not a lot of time, but I don't like waking up in the morning! And my first lesson is at 9, so I don't want to be late.

1 This person ...

A is usually late for school.
B always has breakfast.
C likes to wake up early.

My mum always makes my lunch for me to take to school. I love that, because I don't like the food at school at all and I never eat it. And my friends never eat it, so we all bring our lunch to school. It's funny – we eat our lunch in the canteen, but we don't eat the food they've got there!

2 This student ...

A eats the food in the school canteen.
B eats his friends' lunches.
C eats lunch with his friends in the school canteen.

I've got three afternoon activities. On Tuesdays, I have basketball. I play with my friends and we have a nice time. My afternoon activity on Wednesdays is piano lessons. I like them because I like to spend time with the teacher. She's really great! On Thursdays, I have the maths club. I like it because maths is my favourite subject at school.

3 This student likes the ...

A sports teacher.
B maths teacher.
C music teacher.

My parents, my brother and I get home at different times every day. I usually get home around 4.30pm. My mum comes to school to get me in the car. My brother's school is near our house, so he walks. He gets home at 4. My dad gets home from work around 7. We get home at different times, but we eat dinner at the same time – 8pm, every night!

4 Who gets home first?

A the writer
B the writer's brother
C the writer's dad

My two sisters do a lot of the same things together in the evenings. Melissa, who's 13, and Jessica, who's 14, often watch TV together. They play computer games together too. I sometimes play computer games with them, but I never watch TV with them. Melissa and Jessica always do their homework together, but I never do homework with them.

5 Which activity does the writer do with his sisters?

A his homework
B computer games
C watching TV

Wordpower!

2 **Each of the words in bold is in the wrong sentence. Write a word in bold from another sentence to replace the incorrect one.**

1 I usually write my **uniform** at the weekend. __________
2 Does Daniel's mum **chat** him to school? __________
3 Jessica and Denise **do** their emails every morning. __________
4 Do you **ring** with friends online a lot? __________
5 The kids **check** what they wear to school. __________
6 They **drive** their homework at 8pm. __________
7 I don't wear a **blog** to school. __________
8 When does your alarm clock **choose**? __________

3 **Write a word from the box in each gap to complete the text about school days.**

blog • chat • check • choose • do • drives • rings • send • spend • uniform

SCHOOL DAYS

My school days start early! My alarm clock (1) __________ at 7am and I get out of bed right away. I have a shower and I get ready for my day. I wear a school (2) __________ at my school, so I don't (3) __________ what to wear. If I have time, I (4) __________ my emails to see if I have new ones and I usually (5) __________ a text message to my best friend Lisa. My mum sometimes (6) __________ me to school, but I usually walk. My first lesson starts at 9, I finish at 4 and I get home around 4.30. When I get home, I (7) __________ my homework and then I play basketball with my brother. After that, I (8) __________ with friends online for a while. Finally, I do my favourite thing of the day – I write my (9) __________! It's great fun and I usually (10) __________ an hour online writing it, sometimes more!

Grammar 1

G

Present simple
Look again at *Grammar database 1* on page 146 before doing these exercises.

1 Choose the correct word or phrase.

1 Paul **bring / brings** his lunch to school.
2 I **do / does** my homework every night at 7.
3 My sister and I **live / lives** near our school.
4 Susan doesn't **spend / spends** a lot of time online.
5 **Do you / You do** like to wake up early in the morning?
6 I **doesn't / don't** have breakfast before school.
7 **Does / Do** her dad drive her to school every day?
8 They **gets / get** dressed in their uniforms after their shower.

2 Write a verb from the box in each gap in the present simple.

bring • do • eat • get • go • spend • stay • watch

www.kidblog.co.uk

My sister and I are very different. She often (1) _________ up early, but I don't. I (2) _________ in bed and sleep late. She (3) _________ her lunch to school, but I (4) _________ in the canteen. She (5) _________ a lot of time online every day. I don't like computers, so I usually (6) _________ TV or play sport. She (7) _________ her homework in the kitchen. I do my homework in my bedroom. And finally, she (8) _________ to bed early. And guess what? I don't!

3 Write questions.

1 you / play / football / after school — *Do you play football after school?*
2 Beth / have / breakfast / every morning — _________
3 they / ride / bikes / to school — _________
4 the students / read / your blog — _________
5 they / do / their homework / every night — _________
6 Henry / go / to bed / at midnight — _________
7 you / wear / a uniform / to school / every day — _________
8 Tom and Erin / go / to the cinema / at the weekends — _________

4 Complete the short answers.

1 Do you have a dance class? — No, _________.
2 Does Henry buy snacks at school? — Yes, _________.
3 Do I need a mobile phone to send text messages? — Yes, _________.
4 Does Mike watch TV with his parents? — No, _________.
5 Do they go to school at 8am? — No, _________.
6 Do you do your homework before dinner? — Yes, _________.

Wordpower!

1 **Choose the correct meaning for each phrasal verb.**

1 get back: **leave the house / stop sleeping / come home**
2 turn off: **start a computer / stop sleeping / stop a light**
3 turn on: **start a light / leave the bed / stop a computer**
4 wake up: **stop sleeping / come home / start a light**
5 go out: **come home / leave your bed / leave the house**
6 get up: **stop sleeping / leave the house / leave your bed**

2 **Write a phrasal verb from the box in each gap.**

get back • get up • go out • turn off • turn on • wake up

1 My alarm clock rings at 6.40am, and I ________ and get out of bed.
2 Do you want to ________ tonight, or do you want to stay in?
3 I can't see. Can you ________ the light?
4 I spend an hour online, then I ________ the computer and go to bed.
5 I don't always ________ when my alarm clock rings. Sometimes I just stay in bed.
6 School ends at 3.30pm, but I don't ________ home until 5pm.

Listening

1

1 **➲ KET You will hear George and Elizabeth talking about school life. Match the people to the activities. Write a letter a–f next to each person. There is one letter you do not need to use.**

1 George ___	**a** dance
2 Elizabeth ___	**b** piano
3 Lacy ___	**c** basketball
4 Fran ___	**d** football
5 Kevin ___	**e** chess
	f guitar

Grammar 2 G

Present simple and present continuous

Look again at *Grammar database 2* on page 146 before doing these exercises.

1 Choose the correct word or phrase.

1 Sally and I **play / are playing** a computer game right now.
2 My dad **drives / is driving** his car to work every morning.
3 We **go / are going** to a photography club every Tuesday and Wednesday.
4 I **don't do / am not doing** my homework at the moment.
5 **Are you chatting / Do you chat** with friends online now?
6 What **do your parents usually do / are your parents usually doing** at the weekend?
7 Hi, Robert! What **do you do / are you doing** at the moment?
8 They **aren't having / don't have** their lunch right now.

2 Choose the correct verb. Then put the verbs into the present continuous to complete the sentences.

1 Mike ________________ (**chat / go / win**) his game at the moment.
2 Sheila ________________ (**not go / not get / not take**) to bed now.
3 Michael ________________ (**write / do / make**) a letter right now.
4 They ________________ (**check / live / walk**) to school at the moment.
5 Linda ________________ (**play / win / have**) the piano right now.
6 I ________________ (**read / go / learn**) a great book at the moment.

3 Put the verbs into the correct form (present simple or present continuous) to complete the sentences.

Marsha (1) ________________ (**usually / get**) up at 9am on Saturdays. Then, she (2) ________________ (**always / have**) breakfast. She (3) ________________ (**not / leave**) the house early on Saturdays, so she has time to eat. At the moment, she (4) ________________ (**get**) dressed to go down and have some eggs.

Mark (5) ________________ (**always / go**) to Ben's house at the weekend. Right now, they (6) ________________ (**play**) computer games. Mark (7) ________________ (**usually / win**), but at the moment, he (8) ________________ (**not / win**). Ben is quite happy about that!

Dana (9) ________________ (**chat**) with her friend online at the moment. She (10) ________________ (**spend**) about an hour online every night. At the moment, she and her friend (11) ________________ (**talk**) about their school day. Her friend (12) ________________ (**tell**) her about her dance class.

✔ Quick check

4 Choose the correct answer.

1 Do we use the present simple to talk about things that never happen? **yes / no**
2 Do we use the present continuous to talk about things that happen sometimes? **yes / no**
3 Which one is correct? **I'm reading at night. / I read at night. / both**
4 Which one is correct? **I'm eating now. / I eat now. / both**
5 Do we use *always, sometimes* and *never* with the present continuous? **yes / no**
6 Do we use *right now, now,* and *at the moment* with the present continuous? **yes / no**

Writing

1 Look at these parts of profiles and choose the correct heading, A, B or C.

1 I spend all of my time with my friends Victoria and Joanne. We do everything together. We have many classes together. We spend a lot of time together at the weekend. And when we're not together, we chat online!

A My interests
B About me
C My best friends

2 I play football with my friends and I read books. I also watch a lot of TV and play computer games. I sometimes chat with friends online. I don't spend a lot of time online, though.

A My best friends
B My interests
C My family

3 I'm Rachel. I'm 13 years old. I live in Brighton and I go to Brighton Secondary School.

A My family
B My interests
C About me

4 My mum is a teacher and my dad works in a bank. I've got one brother and one sister. My brother is 11 years old and he plays the piano. My sister is seven years old and she's got a kitten named Sammy.

A My family
B My friends
C My interests

2 Read the text and for each question, choose the correct answer, A, B or C.

My name is Bill. I'm 14 years old. I'm a student at Royston Secondary School. I live with my mum, my dad, and my brother, Todd. My mum's name is Diane. She's a doctor. My dad's name is Richard. He's a teacher. My brother Todd is nine years old. He plays computer games. He's a great little brother!

I play football in a sports club at school. I also play the guitar in a music club. I like clubs a lot. I read books in my free time and I also read things online. I don't watch TV, and I don't chat online.

My friends are Paul and Tony. We play football in the sports club together and we go to the cinema at the weekend. They're great friends. I have some pictures of us from last weekend. They're really funny! We always have a great time together.

That's all for now. Thanks for reading about me!

1 Where can you read a piece of writing like this?

A in a book
B in a blog
C in a newspaper

2 What does the writer describe?

A things happening right now
B general situations
C things the writer does with his family

2

Having Fun!

Reading

1 ➲ KET Read the four texts and match them to the sentences (a–d).

a These parents are happy about their child's hobby.

b You do not have to buy anything for this hobby.

c A sister and brother were together last weekend.

d He wants more free time to hang out with his friends.

1 ___

A new hobby for you!

Do you love taking photographs?
Do you love making films?
This is the perfect club for you!
Join the new **Kids Camera Club!**
Beginners are welcome!
And here's the good news – you can use OUR cameras!
New members can join this Saturday!

2 ___

write reply send

Hi, Sam,

Sorry I didn't call you last weekend. Did you go to the cinema on Saturday? What did you see? My sister and I went to a concert. We had a great time and we got home very late! (Mum wasn't happy about that!)

Talk later,

Jack

3 ___

No free time

'I want to go skateboarding and I want to play video games. But I always have too much homework,' said 15-year-old Marcos from Brazil. 'It's not right. When my dad was young, he had hobbies – he played football, he collected cool things – but I haven't got time for a hobby.'

So, is this a good thing? No, say many doctors.

4 ___

Dear Mr Green,

My son, Tariq, is in your maths class. I'm sorry, but he didn't do his homework last night because he had a very important music exam. When Tariq was only five we gave him a violin and now he plays very well. His father and I both play music too and we are happy about Tariq. I hope you understand.

Thank you,

Ayse Jani

Wordpower!

2 For each question, choose the correct answer, A, B or C.

1 I am a ____ of a swimming club and I swim every weekend.

A hobby
B member
C sport

2 I usually ____ with my cousins at the weekend because we are all the same age.

A hang out
B enjoy
C be

3 Last year, I ____ a new basketball club and I love it!

A joined
B played
C surfed

4 Do you ____ anything special? I don't, but my sister has lots of little cars.

A find
B take
C collect

5 I play ____ nearly every night! Is that a bad thing to do?

A hobbies
B video games
C free time

6 When I play the guitar, it sounds really bad. I'm a ____!

A member
B club
C beginner

7 'Have you got a special ____?'
'Yes, I take photographs!'

A free time
B hobby
C video game

8 She loves going to the cinema in her ____ and I usually go with her.

A hobby
B free time
C beginner

3 Two friends are talking on the internet. Write a word from the box in each gap to complete the dialogue.

beginner • collect • free time • hang out • hobby joined • member • video games

Lilia: What do you do in your (1) ____________, Paul? Do you play (2) ____________ very often?
Paul: No, not much. I usually (3) ____________ with my friends. Last year, we all (4) ____________ a basketball club and we go there all the time. It's great! My little brother plays too, but he's not very good. He's just a (5) ____________. How about you? Have you got a special (6) ____________?
Lilia: Yes. I (7) ____________ postcards.
Paul: Postcards? Are you a (8) ____________ of a postcard club? That's funny!
Lilia: No! My dad works on a ship and every week he sends me a postcard.
Paul: That's cool.
Lilia: I've got postcards from about one hundred countries!
Paul: Wow!

Grammar 1

G

Past simple: regular and basic irregular forms

Look again at *Grammar database 3* on page 147 before doing these exercises.

1 Put the verbs into the past simple to complete the sentences.

1 Last weekend I ______________ to the cinema with my sister. **go**
2 Hey! ______________ you ______________ all my pizza? **eat**
3 Yesterday my brother ______________ a nice photograph of me. **take**
4 ______________ you ______________ all your homework last night? **do**
5 Last Saturday, my mum ______________ a new car. **buy**
6 The maths test was hard and I ______________ the answers. **not / know**
7 Where ______________ you ______________ your t-shirt from? It's nice. **get**
8 My little brother ______________ at school yesterday. **not / be**

2 Write a verb from the box in each gap in the past simple.

be • send • go • buy • take • have

Hello Lilia,

How are you? Well, right now our ship is in Egypt. It's wonderful here. Yesterday I (1) ______________ some free time, so I (2) ______________ to the Pyramids. They (3) ______________ amazing. I (4) ______________ lots of photos and of course I (5) ______________ this postcard for you! I (6) ______________ an email to you last night. Did you get it?

OK, bye for now.

Lots of love,

Dad

3 Complete the questions and match them to the answers (a–f).

1 ______________ you go to the cinema yesterday? ___
2 ______________ your dog come to school yesterday? ___
3 ______________ your brother at the concert last Friday? ___
4 ______________ your parents buy a new car last week? ___
5 ______________ your friends at the basketball game? ___
6 ______________ your sister play tennis yesterday? ___

a Yes, he was.
b No, I didn't.
c Yes, she did.
d Yes, they were.
e Yes, it did!
f No, they didn't.

Wordpower!

1 **Complete the sentences with the correct form of the word in bold.**

1 My sister is a very good ____________ . **cycle**
2 My dad loves his camera. He's a ____________ . **photograph**
3 That music is great. Who is the ____________ ? **guitar**
4 Who is a famous football ____________ in your country? **play**
5 I like playing the piano, but I'm not a good ____________ . **piano**
6 Wow! Look at that ____________ ! She's going very fast. **windsurf**
7 All the ____________ were very happy with the new video game. **game**
8 My uncle was a famous ____________ of very old cars. **collect**

2 **Choose the correct word.**

1 'Do you **collect / collector** anything special?'
'Yes, I do. I've got coins from all over the world.'
2 That **violin / violinist** is only 10 years old, but he's amazing!
3 My sister is a really good **skate / skater**.
4 How many **plays / players** are there in a basketball team?
5 Listen to him! He's a fantastic **piano / pianist**.
6 My brother isn't a good **surfs / surfer**.
7 Is your dad a famous **golf / golfer**?
8 Do you know this **painter / paint**?

Listening

2

1 **You will hear four students talking about the clubs they decided to join. Match the speakers with the club they chose.**

1 Elena ___	**a** the model aeroplane club
2 Nick ___	**b** the dance club
3 Dan ___	**c** the cinema club
4 Linda ___	**d** the football club

2

2 **Listen again and choose the correct word or phrase.**

1 Elena loves **video games / skateboarding**.
2 Nick is a really bad **pianist / guitarist**.
3 Nick goes **windsurfing / skateboarding** all the time.
4 Dan plays **sports / the piano** at the weekend.
5 Dan's sister was in the **cinema club / model aeroplane club** last year.
6 Linda loves **video games / surfing**.
7 All Linda's friends are **gamers / dancers**.
8 Linda's dance teacher said **they are / they aren't** doing the same show.

Grammar 2 G

Past simple: further irregular forms

Look again at *Grammar database 4* on page 147 before doing these exercises.

1 Put the verbs in bold into the past simple to complete the sentences.

1 Last week, my friend Ken ____________ me about a new video game. **tell**
2 Michael's sister ____________ her video game on the internet. **buy**
3 Look! I ____________ this money in my bag! **find**
4 We ____________ hours playing the game. **spend**
5 I ____________ a beautiful picture of my cat yesterday. **draw**
6 My brother ____________ a lot of money for his skateboard. **pay**
7 My uncle and my dad ____________ our house 10 years ago. **build**
8 'Please stop talking!' our teacher ____________. **say**
9 Last night, my sister and I ____________ a huge pizza. **eat**
10 Yesterday my football team ____________ their game. **win**

2 For each question, choose the correct answer, A, B or C.

1 I ___ wake up early this morning.
A not
B didn't
C wasn't

2 My teacher ___ school early today.
A didn't leave
B weren't left
C not left

3 Bad news! Our basketball team ___ the game last night!
A lose
B losing
C lost

4 Where ___ that new bike? It's great!
A did you buy
B you bought
C you buy

5 I ___ the answer to three questions in our test last week.
A not know
B didn't know
C don't know

6 We didn't ___ for the concert. It was free!
A paid
B pay
C paying

3 Write a verb from the box in each gap in the past simple.

bring • hit • leave • spend • teach • tell

1 I ____________ many hours with my cousins last weekend.
2 I ____________ my sister how to take good photographs.
3 Eva ____________ the party early.
4 My friend ____________ his new skateboard to school.
5 My friends ____________ me about the concert last weekend.
6 The player ____________ the ball very well.

✔ Quick check

4 Put a line through the incorrect sentence.

1 I join a new club last week. /
I joined a new club last week.
2 My family didn't went to the cinema last night. /
My family didn't go to the cinema last night.
3 Did you write to your cousin? /
Did you wrote to your cousin?
4 My friends have fun last night. /
My friends had fun last night.
5 My sister bought a new skateboard yesterday. /
My sister buy a new skateboard yesterday.

Writing

Look at these sentences with short forms. We often use short forms in an informal email.

I did not go to the cinema. = I didn't go to the cinema.
The film was not funny. = The film wasn't funny.

1 Read the sentences and rewrite them using the short form.

1 I was not home last night. ______
2 The shops were not open yesterday. ______
3 We did not have much free time today. ______
4 My favourite teacher was not at school on Tuesday. ______
5 I did not send the email to you last week. ______
6 My dad did not collect things when he was young. ______

2 Read this email from Jack to Olga. Look at the words in bold and write the short form.

write reply send

To: Mike Jones <mikejo58@fastmail.com>
Subject: Last weekend

Hi! How are you?

I've got some great news! A few days ago my mum bought me a new guitar – a red one. I love it! (1) **It is** really cool. In my free time, I play my guitar for hours every day and yesterday I joined a music club.

I had a great weekend. (2) **There is** a new cinema near my house so my friends and I went there on Saturday night. After the film, we had something to eat and then we got home very late! My dad (3) **was not** happy about that, so on Sunday I stayed at home. I did all my homework (and I (4) **did not** play any video games!).

In your email last week you told me about a rock concert on Saturday night. Did you go? Did you have a good time? Was the music good? Did your brother take you there?

OK, (5) **I have** got lots of homework to do now!

Write soon!

Love,

Jack

1 ______ 4 ______
2 ______ 5 ______
3 ______

3 Read the email again and for each question, choose the correct answer, A, B or C.

1 In the first paragraph, Jack tells Olga about ...
A his school.
B his family.
C his new hobby.

2 In the second paragraph, Jack writes about ...
A his school.
B his weekend.
C his parents.

3 In the third paragraph, what does Jack ask Olga about?
A her weekend
B her hobbies
C her family

4 Describe the closing expression Jack uses.
A It is friendly.
B It is formal.
C It is unfriendly.

Check your progress! | Units 1–2

1 **Read the text and for each question, choose the correct answer, A, B or C.**

I always (1) ___ early during the week, but never at the weekend. My alarm clock doesn't even (2) ___! At the weekend, I sleep late and enjoy my (3) ___ doing what I want! I like to (4) ___ with friends and do sport. I'm a (5) ___, so I go for bike rides in the afternoon. I'm also a (6) ___ of a sports club. I stay there for a few hours and I (7) ___ home in the afternoon. Then my friends and I (8) ___ for a pizza or a movie at night. And how have I got all this time at the weekend for fun? Well, I (9) ___ all my homework during the week, so my weekends are free!

	A	B	C
1	**A** turn on	**B** wake up	**C** turn off
2	**A** ring	**B** choose	**C** check
3	**A** hobby	**B** beginner	**C** free time
4	**A** hang out	**B** join	**C** collect
5	**A** guitarist	**B** pianist	**C** cyclist
6	**A** gamer	**B** member	**C** surfer
7	**A** go out	**B** get up	**C** get back
8	**A** wake up	**B** hang out	**C** go out
9	**A** make	**B** do	**C** go

9 marks

2 **Put the verbs into the correct form (present simple or present continuous) to complete the text.**

Mary and Donna are sisters, but they often (10) ___________ (**do**) different things in their free time. Mary (11) ___________ (**enjoy**) reading books. At the moment, she (12) ___________ (**read**) a book about cats. Donna, however, (13) ___________ (**not like**) books. She usually (14) ___________ (**play**) the piano in her free time. She (15) ___________ (**not take**) piano lessons right now. Her mother is a pianist, so they often (16) ___________ (**sit**) together at the piano and she (17) ___________ (**help**) Donna with her music.

8 marks

3 **Put the verbs into the past simple to complete the sentences.**

18 Kevin and John ___________ (**be**) at football practice last night.
19 Jenny ___________ (**take**) some fantastic photos on her holiday last summer.
20 ___________ (**you / go**) to the cinema with Michelle and Linda yesterday?
21 We ___________ (**play**) video games with Gary and Rob last week.
22 Helen ___________ (**bring**) the best gift to Paula's birthday party.
23 I ___________ (**not / write**) my blog at all yesterday afternoon.
24 They ___________ (**build**) a very large model aeroplane at the weekend.
25 Henry ___________ (**spend**) many hours online on Tuesday evening.

8 marks

Total: ___ / 25 marks

3

Tell me a Story!

Reading

1 **KET Read this extract from a science fiction story and for each question, choose the correct answer, A, B or C.**

>>>>>>>>>>>>>>>>>>>>>>>>>>>>

Captain Lawrence was looking at the amazing view from his spacecraft. It was the alien planet Xen. It took him seven years to travel this far, and now he was here.

He was happy because it was a big moment, and not just for him, but for his crew. But he was also worried. He knew there were aliens on the planet, and he didn't want the crew to have problems.

The spacecraft was landing when the captain gave the last instructions. 'First Officer Michaels, get ready to open the door. Second Officer Daniels, stand behind him. Watch for aliens. And remember ... be careful!' said the captain.

While First Officer Michaels was leaving the spacecraft, he saw three aliens coming to the spacecraft. The aliens stopped a few metres in front of the spacecraft. 'Captain, I don't know about this. These aliens seem terrible,' said Michaels.

Just then, Daniels screamed, 'Be careful! Three aliens right behind you!' The three aliens took Michaels from the spacecraft. When the captain saw that he was in trouble, he ran out of the spacecraft. He had to help his crew.

1 Captain Lawrence travelled for 10 years to get to Xen.
A Right
B Wrong
C Doesn't say

2 Both the captain and his crew were happy about the end of the trip.
A Right
B Wrong
C Doesn't say

3 His crew was worried about the aliens before they landed.
A Right
B Wrong
C Doesn't say

4 The captain gave instructions as the spacecraft landed.
A Right
B Wrong
C Doesn't say

5 The aliens stopped a few metres in front of the spacecraft.
A Right
B Wrong
C Doesn't say

6 Michaels was worried that the aliens were not nice.
A Right
B Wrong
C Doesn't say

7 Daniels screamed when he saw the aliens.
A Right
B Wrong
C Doesn't say

8 Captain Lawrence stayed in the ship all the time.
A Right
B Wrong
C Doesn't say

Wordpower!

2 Choose the correct word for each definition.

1 This happens when you can't see something that was there before. **appear / disappear**
2 This is the time when you are seven years old. **childhood / adventure**
3 This is the opposite of 'normal'. **terrible / strange**
4 This describes how you feel when something is not right. **disappeared / worried**
5 If you see something far way, you see it in the **hide / distance.**
6 This describes something that's bad. **worried / terrible**
7 This is when you look at something for the first time. **hide / notice**
8 This means something happened because of bad luck. **unfortunately / thoughtfully**

3 Write a word from the box in each gap to complete the text.

childhood • disappeared • distance • notice
strange • terrible • unfortunately • worried

I remember a story I read in my (1) ______________ . It was an adventure story about pirates. In the story, the pirates helped people. I thought that was (2) ______________ . I always thought that pirates were very bad and they did (3) ______________ things to people. The story was about a group of people who were (4) ______________ because of a bad man who lived on their island. That man made them work all the time and (5) ______________ , he didn't give them any money. One day, the pirates came to the island. The man didn't (6) ______________ them when they arrived and the pirates took him away in their ship. The people of the island were very happy. They all climbed to the top of the hill to see the pirates' ship in the (7) ______________ as it left. When the ship (8) ______________ , they had a big party.

4 Each of the words in bold is in the wrong sentence. Write a word in bold from another sentence to replace the incorrect one.

1 I can see something very dark and scary in the **childhood**.

____

2 Leslie was **unfortunately** about the man returning to her front door.

____

3 Did you **disappeared** that the window was open when we got home?

____

4 She's got many wonderful memories from her **distance**.

____

5 A woman was standing in front of me, but then she **notice**.

____

6 Did you hear that **worried** noise coming from the kitchen?

____

7 She wanted to leave the room but **strange** the door was closed.

____

Grammar 1 G

Past simple and past continuous

Look again at *Grammar database 5* on page 148 before doing these exercises.

1 Correct the words or phrases in bold.

1 Mary walked to the window when she **was hearing** the strange noise. ______
2 John **read** his science fiction book when Matt called. ______
3 I was talking on the phone when Jenny **was arriving**. ______
4 Michael was walking when the man **was jumping** in front of him. ______
5 The detective asked what Simon **did** from 5pm to 6pm. ______
6 The man **was coming** through the window as Jill was sleeping. ______
7 Mark **wrote** in his diary when Helen called. ______
8 Sarah fell and hurt her arm while she **ran** down the street. ______

2 Choose the correct word or phrase.

Wendy (1) **was doing / did** the dishes when she heard a scream. She ran to the window to see what happened. She didn't notice anything strange while she (2) **looked / was looking** out the window. She (3) **was deciding / decided** to go outside to find out what happened. While she (4) **was walking / walked** to the front door, she picked up her mobile phone. She was ready to call the police if something terrible happened. When she (5) **was arriving / arrived** in her front garden, she heard the scream again. It was coming from her neighbour's house. She (6) **was walking / walked** to their house. When her neighbour (7) **opened / was opening** the door, Wendy saw what was happening. Her neighbour (8) **watched / was watching** a film and the screams were coming from the TV!

3 ➲ KET Read the story about a family trip. For each question, choose the correct answer, A, B or C.

Jason and his family (1) ___ to go on a 'ghost holiday' in England. They (2) ___ to Pluckley, a town that's home to 13 ghosts. While they (3) ___ there, Jason saw a figure of a woman in the forest. She was staring at their car while she (4) ___ above the ground. Jason told his dad, 'Stop the car! It's one of the ghosts!' When Jason's dad (5) ___ the car, the woman disappeared. While they (6) ___ in the town, the people in the village told Jason's family about the 'screaming forest' a place with 'lost' ghosts. They went there one evening before dark. Nothing happened at first. Then, while the wind (7) ___, Jason heard a voice. 'Did you hear that? Someone is saying, "Jaaa-sssooon!"'

His mum replied, 'Yes, that's your sister!' She was standing behind Jason, and when he (8) ___ around, she started to laugh!

	A	B	C
1	**A** were deciding	**B** decided	**C** was deciding
2	**A** was going	**B** go	**C** went
3	**A** were driving	**B** was driving	**C** drove
4	**A** were floating	**B** float	**C** was floating
5	**A** was stopping	**B** were stopping	**C** stopped
6	**A** were staying	**B** stayed	**C** was staying
7	**A** blew	**B** was blowing	**C** were blowing
8	**A** was turning	**B** were turning	**C** turned

Wordpower!

1 **Each of the words in bold is in the wrong sentence. Write a word in bold from another sentence to replace the incorrect one.**

1 Mary looked **about** the strange man across the street.
____

2 They laughed **for** the funny story.
____

3 What did you and Lucy talk **at** the other day?
____

4 Do you ever think **to** life on other planets?
____

5 She asked her dad **at** some money to buy a book.
____

6 Did you talk **about** Bill when you saw him?
____

2 **KET** **Write a word in each gap to complete the email.**

write reply send

To: Ben Smith <ben.smith@fastmail.com>
Subject: Liam's present

Hi, Ben!

Thanks (1) _____________ your email. I was thinking (2) _____________ an adventure book for Liam's birthday. It's called *Lost Treasure*. I was looking (3) _____________ it yesterday. I laughed (4) _____________ some of the stories in it. Let's talk (5) _____________ it when we see each other tomorrow. We can go to the bookshop (6) _____________ Fran. She knows many good books. She can tell us what book to buy (7) _____________ Liam. Oh, and don't worry, I asked my mum (8) _____________ drive us to the party.

Bye!

Beth

Listening

3

1 **Listen to two friends talking. Write a word or short phrase in each gap to complete the sentences.**

1 Angela and her brother were _____________ when they heard someone at the door.
2 Angela's brother thought the strange thing was probably a(n) _____________ .
3 While Angela was standing in the _____________, she saw something.
4 Angela saw a man when she _____________ the light.
5 When their dog saw the man, he started to make _____________ sounds.
6 Angela's parents were at the _____________ when the strange thing happened.

Grammar 2 G

Imperative, infinitives, *-ing* form

Look again at *Grammar database 6* on page 148 before doing these exercises.

1 Put the verbs into the full infinitive or *-ing* form to complete the sentences.

1 They chose ____________ (**read**) a book about spacecraft.
2 Do you remember ____________ (**visit**) that strange house last night?
3 John told the man to stop ____________ (**look**) into his kitchen window.
4 They plan ____________ (**go**) on an exciting adventure this summer.
5 She forgot ____________ (**close**) the door when she left the house.
6 Do they enjoy ____________ (**stay**) in hotels with ghosts?

2 Make the sentences into instructions using the imperative.

1 She told her to put the book down.
Put the book down!

2 He told her not to open the door.
____

3 Her mum told her to do her homework.
____

4 She told him to read the story again.
____

5 The teacher told the students not to talk in class.
____

6 She told him to turn off the lights.
____

3 ➲ KET Read the detective story and for each question, choose the correct answer, A, B or C.

The policeman wanted to know what happened in the shop. '(1) ___ for me what you saw,' he said to Anne. Anne promised (2) ___ him everything. She said she saw a man (3) ___ out of the shop, but he stopped at the front door when some money (4) ___ out of his hand. She watched him (5) ___ it up and put it in his coat. She heard him (6) ___ something, and just after that, a man who worked in the shop came to the front. '(7) ___ that man!' he cried. She was scared and she didn't say anything. Just then, a big black car came and the man ran to the car. She saw him (8) ___ in the car. 'It was a terrible moment. I hope you get that bad man!' Anne said. The policeman replied, 'Don't worry, I have all the information I need.'

	A	B	C
1	**A** You describe	**B** Describe	**C** To describe
2	**A** telling	**B** tell	**C** to tell
3	**A** run	**B** running	**C** to run
4	**A** was falling	**B** to fall	**C** fell
5	**A** pick	**B** picking	**C** to pick
6	**A** to say	**B** say	**C** saying
7	**A** Don't stop	**B** You stop	**C** Stop
8	**A** got	**B** get	**C** to get

Quick check

4 Choose the correct answer.

1 Do we use the imperative to tell people to do things? **yes / no**
2 Do we usually use the full infinitive after *enjoy*, *finish*, and *miss*? **yes / no**
3 Which is correct? **She began to tell her. / She began telling her. / both**
4 Do we use the past simple for situations in progress? **yes / no**
5 Do we use the past continuous for situations in progress at a particular time in the past? **yes / no**
6 Which is correct? **He was working at 1pm. / He worked at 1pm. / both**

Writing

1 Read the story and match each part of the story with a statement.

1 A different kind of treasure ___	**a** This tells us what James said.
2 Paragraph 1 ___	**b** This tells us what James found by following the map.
3 Paragraph 2 ___	**c** This tells us what James did with the map.
4 Paragraph 3 ___	**d** This tells us what the title is.
5 Paragraph 4 ___	**e** This tells us when the story happened.

A different kind of treasure

(1) I was walking home from school on a Thursday afternoon when I found a strange map. It was a map of my village, and there was an 'X' on the map. Next to the 'X' were the words 'TREASURE HERE!'

(2) After I thought about it for a few minutes, I decided to look for this treasure. The place with the 'X' was not far from my house. I walked for a few minutes, and when I got to the street where the 'X' was, I started to hear music.

(3) I continued to walk down the street. When I arrived at the house, I saw some people in the front garden. They were standing near a table with a cake that had gold coins around it. Then, I saw my friend Carrie. 'Hi, James! You found the party! Come and have some cake!' Carrie said to me.

(4) 'Party? I didn't know you were having a party! Why does this map say there's treasure? Where did you get all these gold coins?' When Carrie heard my questions, she started to laugh. She said the gold coins weren't real and the treasure was the party. It was all just a joke. I guess it was a good way to get people to go to the party!

2 Read the story again and for each question, choose the correct answer, A, B or C.

1 How many examples of the past continuous can you find?
A 1
B 2
C 3

2 Which paragraphs have got examples of words people have said?
A Paragraphs 1, 3 and 4 only
B Paragraphs 1, 2, 3 and 4
C Paragraphs 3 and 4 only

3 Which paragraph has got an example of the imperative?
A Paragraph 1
B Paragraph 2
C Paragraph 3

4

Let's Celebrate!

Reading

1 ➲ KET Read the four texts and match them to the sentences (a–d).

a You do not have to organise your own party.
b A parent is going to have a nice surprise.
c Someone's room does not look good.
d There's a serious problem between two friends.

1 ___

Hi, Mum,

I'm not home because I've gone to Mike's house. There's something wrong with his computer and I think I know what to do.
I'm really REALLY sorry that I haven't tidied up my room yet, but I promise I will tidy it up when I get back. Don't worry! See you in about two hours. (I ate all the pizza on the table – was it for me?)

2 ___

Hi, Fred,

Have you heard the news? David has just had a big fight with his best friend, Kevin. They are both guitarists in the same band and last weekend while they were playing at a concert, Dave just left! Can you believe it – in the middle of a concert! Not cool! I haven't heard the full story yet, so I don't know what happened – but everyone is talking about it.

3 ___

write reply send

Dad,

I've just called Mum and she hasn't left the office yet. Everything is ready! We've already put up the decorations and we've made a birthday card, too. Everything looks great, but we haven't bought the birthday cake yet. We ordered it last week, so it will be ready. Can you get it on your way home now? Hurry! Mum will be home soon. She's going to get a big surprise!

Laura

4 ___

★★★★★★★★★★★★★★★★★★★★★★★★★

Celebrate your birthday in a different way!
Call **The Perfect Party People!**
Would you like to have the **Perfect Party** indoors? Call us! Outdoors? Call us!
Have you sent the invitations yet? **No?**
Have you ordered refreshments and snacks yet? **No?**
You have fun with your guests and we do all the work!
The Perfect Party People are here for **You!!!**
contact us: info@theperfectpartypeople.com

★★★★★★★★★★★★★★★★★★★★★★★★★

Wordpower!

2 Choose the correct answer, A, B or C.

1 It's a beautiful day. Let's have lunch ____ .
A cheap
B popular
C outdoors

2 Everyone loves that music. It's very ____ with young people.
A order
B popular
C indoors

3 It's raining today so let's stay at home and play games ____ .
A indoors
B reply
C cheap

4 I think I will ____ a big pizza for lunch today. I'm very hungry!
A arrive
B order
C reply

5 Sorry, I can't hang out with you after school. I have to ____ my room.
A tidy up
B reply
C outdoors

6 Those CDs are really ____ so let's buy two!
A indoors
B cheap
C arrive

7 What time will the guests ____ ? Not before 8pm, I hope.
A reply
B popular
C arrive

8 I invited Paul to my party, but I haven't had a ____ from him yet.
A order
B reply
C cheap

3 Write a word from the box in each gap to complete the email.

arrive • cheap • indoors • order • outdoors
popular • reply • tidy up

write reply send

To: Andreas007@andreas.com
Subject: Concert at school

Hi, Andreas!

How are you? I'm so tired!!! Last week my class organised a concert at school. Everyone wanted to have the concert (1) ________ but our teachers were worried about the rain, so finally we decided to have it (2) ________ . There's a band in our town that is very (3) ________ .They played and everybody liked them. We also sold tickets to the concert, but they were very (4) ________ so a lot of people brought their friends from other schools. We had a little café too where people could (5) ________ refreshments. The concert finished at midnight and then we had to (6) ________ . It took forever! I didn't (7) ________ home until two in the morning! Hey – did you get that new video game? I haven't had a (8) ________ from you yet. I'm waiting for an invitation to come and play it at your house!

C u soon,

Peter

Grammar 1 G

Present perfect simple 1

Look again at *Grammar database 7* on page 148 before doing these exercises.

1 **For each question, choose the correct answer, A, B or C.**

1 Have you ___ sent the invitations?
A never **B** yet **C** already

2 I haven't had any replies about the party ___ .
A already **B** ye **C** ever

3 Peter ___ tidied up the room yet. It looks terrible!
A wasn't **B** haven't **C** hasn't

4 ___ you told Jenny about the party?
A Did **B** Have **C** Were

5 Hey! Who has ___ my dinner?
A eat **B** ate **C** eaten

6 Yes, I'm free to meet you now! I've ___ finished my homework!
A just **B** yet **C** only

2 **Write a word in each gap to complete the note from Maria to her brother, Sam.**

ago • already • has • hasn't
Have • haven't • just • yet

Sam,

Can you do something for me, PLEASE?! I need some help organising my party. I (1) ___ sent all the invitations (2) ___ . Can you send them for me? You need to open my computer and send them from my email. OK? I've (3) ___ made the invitations – but I have to stay late at school today and I want to send them today!

If you have any problems, call me! Did you talk to your friend about the music? (4) ___ you had a reply yet? I hope he (5) ___ forgotten about my party! His CDs are great. By the way, I've (6) ___ spoken to Mum. She called me two minutes (7) ___ and GOOD news: your new video game (8) ___ arrived.

Bye!

Wordpower!

1 **Choose the correct word.**

Jane: Ben, what do you do in your free time? Have you got an (1) **interested / interesting** hobby?

Ben: No, not really, but I like music.

Jane: What about films? Are you (2) **interesting / interested** in films?

Ben: Yes, I saw a movie last weekend that was (3) **amazing / amazed**. My mum came with me, but she didn't like it. She thought the film was very (4) **frightened / frightening**! She had her eyes closed all the time!

2 **Write a word in each gap to complete the sentences. The first letter is given to help you.**

1 I enjoyed this book; I thought it was really **i**__________.
2 It was a **f**__________ film about ghosts. I screamed a couple of times!
3 Wow! He's an **a**__________ basketball player.
4 I'm so **e**__________ about going to the party tonight!
5 Are you **i**__________ in animals?
6 I am **a**__________ that I did so well in the test because it was really hard.

Listening

4

1 **KET Listen to Tim and his mother talking on the telephone and for each question, choose the correct answer, A, B or C.**

1 Tim sent the invitations last ...

A Tuesday.
B Thursday.
C Saturday.

2 How many invitations did he send?

A 13
B 15
C 50

3 How many replies has he had?

A 50
B 30
C 13

4 What food has he ordered?

A pizza
B ice cream
C sandwiches

5 What decorations has he decided to use?

A lights
B balloons
C flowers

Grammar 2 G

Present perfect simple 2

Look again at *Grammar database 8* on page 149 before doing these exercises.

1 **Look at the information about what Eva, Jim and Mark have done (✔) or haven't done (✘) in their lives. Then put the verbs into the present perfect simple to complete the sentences.**

		 Japanese food		
Eva	✘	✘	✔	✘
Jim	✔	✔	✘	✔
Mark	✔	✔	✔	✘

1 Jim ___has eaten___ Japanese food. **eat**
2 Jim and Mark ______ a horse. **ride**
3 Eva ______ a dolphin. **see**
4 Mark and Jim ______ Japanese food. **eat**
5 Jim ______ to New York. **be**
6 Mark and Eva ______ a dolphin. **see**

2 **Look at the information again. Write a word in each gap to complete the questions and answer them.**

1 ___Has___ Jim ___seen___ a dolphin? ___Yes, he has.___
2 ______ Mark and Jim ______ a horse? ______
3 ______ Eva ______ a horse? ______
4 ______ Mark ______ Japanese food? ______
5 ______ Jim ______ to New York? ______
6 ______ Eva ______ Japanese food? ______
7 ______ Eva ______ to New York? ______

✔ Quick check

3 **Put a line through the incorrect sentence.**

1 I saw Kevin at the party last night. / I have seen Kevin at the party last night.
2 I haven't tidied my room yet. / I wasn't tidying my room yet.
3 'Have you ever been to London?'
'No, I haven't.' / 'No, I didn't.'
4 My dad just has bought a new car! / My dad has just bought a new car!
5 I not have had dinner yet. / I haven't had dinner yet.

Writing

Look at these questions that begin with the word *can*.
We often use *can* to ask for something in a friendly way.

Can you help me?
Can you decorate the room with me?

These sentences are not very friendly.

Help me with the party!
Bring your CDs to the party!

1 Read the sentences and say if they are friendly (F) or not friendly (NF).

1 Help me tidy up this room now! NF
2 Can you bring your guitar to the party? ___
3 Can you help me organise the party? ___
4 Buy a cake! ___
5 Can you call me tonight? ___
6 Take all the chairs outdoors! ___

2 Read this note from Michelle to her friend Liam. For each question, choose the correct answer, A, B or C.

Dear Liam,

How are you? This is just a quick note to make sure that you got the invitation to my party next week. Did you get it? I hope so! I'm really looking forward to it! I'm sure we'll have a great time. Everyone will be there! Mum said that we can have the party outdoors if it doesn't rain!

I know that you're really busy, but there are two things that I need some help with. The first thing is the music. I know that you play guitar and you are in a band. Can you talk to the other guys in the band to see if they can play at the party? Your music is very popular. Everyone loves it.

The second thing is decorations. I'm not going to have balloons – I want lights. Can I use the lights I saw at one of your concerts a few months ago? They are really pretty and they'll make everything look so nice. I'm sure the guests will like them.

Can you call me tonight so we can talk?

And guess what! I've ordered a huge chocolate cake for the party – and it will look like a guitar!

I've got to go now.

Love,

Michelle

1 Michelle is excited about her party. Which sentence tells us this?
A Everyone will be there!
B I am really looking forward to it!
C I hope so!

2 Michelle knows her friend hasn't got a lot of free time. Which sentence tells us this?
A Can you call me tonight so we can talk?
B And your music is very popular
C I know that you're really busy, but …

3 Michelle asks in a friendly way for help with music. Which sentence does this?
A Can you call me tonight so we can talk?
B Can you please help me with the music?
C The first thing is the music.

4 Michelle asks for help with another thing. What is it?
A the cake
B the decorations
C the invitations

5 Michelle also writes about something special she has ordered for the party? What is it?
A a cake
B the invitations
C decorations

6 When Michelle finishes her note to Liam …
A she is friendly.
B she is not friendly.
C she is sad.

Check your progress! | Units 3–4

1 Read the text and for each question, choose the correct answer, A, B or C.

Everyone has stories from their (1) ___. Some stories are about (2) ___ ghosts and other stories are about (3) ___ adventures. My story is about a birthday party we had for my little brother. Because we had a big garden, we decided to have his party (4) ___. We decorated the garden with lights and big balloons and when the guests (5) ___, they said it looked (6) ___. Everyone was having a good time but I started to feel very (7) ___. I couldn't find my brother! Suddenly, we heard a (8) ___ scream. We looked up and there, in the tree, was my little brother.

	A	B	C
1	**A** distance	**B** childhood	**C** strange
2	**A** unfortunately	**B** frightening	**C** worried
3	**A** cheap	**B** amazed	**C** exciting
4	**A** excited	**B** reply	**C** outdoors
5	**A** arrived	**B** ordered	**C** tidied up
6	**A** popular	**B** excited	**C** amazing
7	**A** notice	**B** worried	**C** unfortunately
8	**A** terrible	**B** interested	**C** cheap

8 marks

2 Write a preposition in each gap to complete the sentences.

9 Look ________ this amazing photograph of the castle.
10 Why is that detective talking ________ our teacher? Has something happened?
11 Shhhh! I don't want to talk ________ that ghost story! It's too frightening!
12 This pizza is fantastic! Let's ask ________ some more!
13 Stop laughing ________ me. I don't like it!

5 marks

3 Put the verbs into the correct form to complete the sentences.

14 While we ____________ (**have**) dinner last night, we ____________ (**hear**) a frightening scream.
15 Yesterday, while I ____________ (**watch**) a science fiction film, my brother started to play his guitar and I ____________ (**tell**) him to stop!
16 What ____________ you ____________ (**do**) at six o'clock last night? I called you three times but you ____________ (**answer**) the phone.
17 While I ____________ (**tidy up**) my room, I ____________ (**find**) my favourite CD from years ago!
18 I promised ____________ (**invite**) all my friends to my party.
19 Do you enjoy ____________ (**read**) adventure stories?

6 marks

4 Write one word or phrase in each gap to complete the text.

20 '________ you ever been to London?' 'No, I ________.'
21 '________ Jenny read that detective story yet?' 'Yes, she ________.'
22 Sorry, I can't meet you today. I ________ done my homework yet.
23 '________ eat food in class!' said the teacher.
24 '________ up your room!' said my mother.
25 Please Dad, ________ me that story about your childhood again.

6 marks

Total: _____ / 25 marks

5

Off we Go!

Reading

1 Quickly read the text and answer the questions.

1 Is the text from a magazine or a school newspaper? ____________

2 Is the text for children or adults? ____________

TRAVEL AND LEARN!

This week in *UK Travel*, writer Jeffrey Smith talks to Ronda Evans, a tour guide for one of London's best travel agencies, Travel London. Ms Evans has been a tour guide for eight years now. She has organised hundreds of tours for Travel London, and she knows all about the best things to do when you're in London.

Jeffrey: What kinds of tours do you organise for Travel London?

Ronda: I do many types of tours. I do bus tours, walking tours, museum tours and boat tours on the River Thames. I take people to important places in London, such as Buckingham Palace and the Houses of Parliament. We go inside the buildings and I talk about what goes on there. I also talk about the history of the place because I really enjoy history.

Jeffrey: Tell us about your favourite type of tour.

Ronda: I think my favourite type of tour is when I've got a group of kids to show around the city. I love children, and when I was young, I loved going on school trips. There are a lot of things to learn about in London. And when children visit London for the first time, it's really amazing to them. They want to know about everything. They never get bored! At Travel London, we try to get parents to come to London with their children. We've got special prices for young kids, so it's a good chance for them to travel and learn at the same time.

Jeffrey: Has Travel London got any new types of tours that people might be interested in?

Ronda: We've recently started cycling tours. We go around the neighbourhoods of London and visit famous places. We go to the usual places that I talked about before. But we also go past the homes of famous people, for example. It's good fun and Travel London provides the bicycles. You travel, learn, and do sport at the same time!

You can learn more about Travel London's exciting tours by calling their offices at 0207 856 5252 or visiting their website at www.travellondontours.co.uk.

2 Read the text again and write a word or phrase from the text to complete the sentences.

1 Ronda Evans has been a tour guide for ____________ years.

2 Ronda enjoys talking about the ____________ of important places.

3 Ronda loved going on ____________ when she was young.

4 Travel London has got special prices for ____________ .

5 Ronda travels past the homes of ____________ on the cycling tour.

Wordpower!

3 ➲ KET For each question, choose the correct answer, A, B or C.

1 Sharon wants to ___ London this year.
A travel
B visit
C stay

2 Her friends went last year and said it was an amazing ___ .
A view
B history
C experience

3 She is going to go on the internet to ___ the tickets this weekend.
A organise
B enjoy
C visit

4 She will look on a website to ___ information on hotels and tours.
A visit
B find out
C spend

5 She hopes the sky will be ___ on the day of the picnic.
A happy
B high
C clear

6 She hopes to ___ the trip and have a lot of fun.
A find out
B enjoy
C visit

4 Write a word from the box in each gap to complete the text.

clear • experience • joy • find • organise • past • trip • view • visit

Thomas and his family are going on a (1) _________ . They plan to (2) _________ Paris during the first week of June. His mum is going to (3) _________ the hotel stay and the plane tickets. She hopes to get a hotel that's got a nice (4) _________ of the Eiffel Tower. His dad is using the internet to (5) _________ out about things to do while they are there. They are going in the summer because the weather is usually nice and (6) _________ during that time. Later today, Thomas is going to a bookshop that he walked (7) _________ the other day. There he will buy a book with all the places the family can (8) _________ . He thinks he and his family will have a terrific (9) _________ that they will remember for a long time.

Grammar 1

G

will* and *be going to

Look again at *Grammar database 9* on page 149 before doing these exercises.

1 For each question, choose the correct answer A, B, or C.

1 They ___ to take a tour of the city.
A is going
B are going
C will

2 I ___ to work at the London Dungeon this summer.
A am going
B will
C won't

3 I'm lost. ___ help me find my hotel?
A You will
B Will you
C You are going to

4 There are no clouds in the sky. It ___ rain soon.
A will
B won't
C is going to

5 'Are you going to take a trip this summer?' 'No, ___.'
A I'm not
B I am
C I won't

6 'Will you call the hotel and book the room?' 'Yes, I ___.'
A won't
B am
C will

2 Write a word from the box in each gap to complete the text.

am • are • aren't • be • going • have • will • won't

My friend Billy and I are (1) ________ to Edinburgh together this summer. Of course, we (2) ________ be going alone. Billy's mum and dad are coming too but Billy and I (3) ________ going to plan each day's activities, so it will be exciting. We both want to go to Edinburgh Castle. That will (4) ________ an interesting experience for sure. We (5) ________ also see some of the other castles in the area. I (6) ________ going to buy a book on Edinburgh today to learn more about it. Billy and I (7) ________ going to take care of the hotel plans. Billy's mum and dad will do that. But I think we're going to leave in June and stay for one week. I think we will (8) ________ a terrific time!

3 Match each question with its answer (a–h).

1 'Is he going to buy the tickets?'	'No, ___.'	**a** they will
2 'Are you going to visit a museum?'	'No, ___.'	**b** they aren't
3 'Will you and Tom stay for a week?'	'No, ___.'	**c** I'm not
4 'Are they going to travel tomorrow?'	'No, ___.'	**d** I will
5 'Will he go on a tour of the city?'	'Yes, ___.'	**e** we are
6 'Are you and Lisa going to leave today?'	'Yes, ___.'	**f** we won't
7 'Will they take the train to Paris?'	'Yes, ___.'	**g** he will
8 'Will you come with us to the beach?'	'Yes, ___.'	**h** he's not

Wordpower!

1 KET **Write a phrase for each description. The first letter is given to help you.**

1 You put this on your face and body. **s** __ __ **c** __ __ __ __
2 This gives you information about a place. **g** __ __ __ __ **b** __ __ __
3 You need one of these to drive a car.
d __ __ __ __ __ __ **l** __ __ __ __ __ __
4 This person takes you to famous places and talks about them.
t __ __ __ **g** __ __ __ __
5 You can go on one of these when you are a pupil.
s __ __ __ __ __ **t** __ __ __
6 You buy this in order to travel by train.
t __ __ __ __ **t** __ __ __ __ __
7 Someone takes you to different places on this kind of trip.
g __ __ __ __ __ **t** __ __ __
8 You use this to buy things. **c** __ __ __ __ __ **c** __ __ __

2 **Choose a phrase from exercise 1 to complete each sentence.**

When Mary was younger, she and her classmates took a (1) ________ to Rome. She really loved it, so she decided to go back with a friend. Last summer, she and her friend Lisa went on a (2) ________ and their group visited all the famous places. There was a (3) ________ with their group that told them about the history of the city. One day, she and Lisa walked around the city without their group. Lisa bought a (4) ________ to help them get around town. After a couple of hours, Mary bought some (5) ________ for her face. She used her (6) ________ to buy it, as she didn't have any money. Later, they wanted to hire a car to drive around, but they didn't have a (7) ________. Instead, they each bought a (8) ________ and took the train to different places. They had a wonderful time!

Listening

5

1 **Listen to the conversation and complete the notes.**

TRIP TO BRIGHTON

Name of hotel in centre: Brighton Hotel
Address: (1) 21 ________ St
Room for one: (2) ________
Phone number: (3) ________
Places to visit: museum and (4) ________
Museum closed on: (5) ________

Grammar 2

G

Talking about the future: present simple and present continuous

Look again at *Grammar database 10* on page 149 before doing these exercises.

1 Choose the correct word or phrase.

1 What time does your plane **land / landing** on Sunday?
2 I'll send you a text message when I **get / am getting** there.
3 They **are staying / stay** in Chicago for a month.
4 The train for London **will leave / leaves** at 9am tomorrow morning.
5 Jason and his dad **is / are** travelling to Berlin on Tuesday.
6 Will you call me as soon as you **arrive / are arriving**?

2 Write a word from the box in each gap to complete the text.

after • are • as • does • leaves • staying

write reply send

Hi, Amy,

I'm excited about your visit this weekend. When (1) ________ your train arrive on Saturday? I know it (2) ________ London at 9am. I've made some plans for Saturday afternoon. We (3) ________ visiting the museum at 11am. We're having lunch at this nice pizza place (4) ________ we leave the museum. Are you (5) ________ for the whole weekend? I hope so! Write back as soon (6) ________ you get this message.

Bethany

3 KET Read the text and for each question, choose the correct answer, A, B or C.

My family and I are (1) ___ to Russia for a holiday. I'm really excited about it because we're (2) ___ for a whole week. We (3) ___ travelling on Monday morning and the plane (4) ___ the airport in London at 6am. I hope I (5) ___ be too tired to wake up! There will be a person from the hotel at the airport when we (6) ___ there. He's (7) ___ to take us to the hotel. My mum has organised the trip well, I must say! On Tuesday, we (8) ___ taking a walking tour of Moscow. It's a good way to learn about the city. I don't know what we're (9) ___ for the rest of the week, but I'm sure it (10) ___ be fun!

	A	B	C
1	**A** go	**B** going	**C** goes
2	**A** stays	**B** stay	**C** staying
3	**A** is	**B** are	**C** will
4	**A** leaving	**B** leaves	**C** leave
5	**A** aren't	**B** not	**C** won't
6	**A** getting	**B** get	**C** gets
7	**A** will	**B** going	**C** go
8	**A** am	**B** is	**C** are
9	**A** does	**B** do	**C** doing
10	**A** will	**B** is	**C** going

Quick check

4 Choose the correct answer.

1 Do we usually use *will* when we make an offer or a request? **yes / no**
2 Do we usually use *be going to* to talk about plans we've already made? **yes / no**
3 Which is correct? **You'll enjoy London. / You're going to enjoy London. / both**
4 Do we use the present simple for timetables and fixed events? **yes / no**
5 Do we use the present simple after time words like *when* and *after*? **yes / no**
6 Which is correct? **We stay for three days. / We're staying for three days. / both**

Writing

1 Read the postcard and choose the correct answer, A, B or C to complete the sentences.

Hi, Stan,

(1) How are you? Are you enjoying your summer holidays? When are you leaving for Spain?

(2) We're here in Athens and it's really fantastic! We've been to many places and we're having a great time. We went to the Acropolis yesterday, which was amazing. It's so beautiful! We also went to the new museum and walked around the old part of the city. Today we're visiting some of the other museums in the city. I'm very excited about that! I'll take lots of pictures for you!

(3) Tomorrow we're leaving Athens. We're going to the Greek islands for five days. I'm going to swim in the sea every day! We get back next week. I'll call you as soon as I get home!

Bye for now!
Your friend,
David

Stan Lively
20 Spencer Road
Newbury
MF1 3GF
UK

1 David asks Stan if he is ...
A enjoying Spain.
B having a nice summer.
C leaving for Spain.

2 Today David is visiting ...
A the Acropolis.
B some museums.
C the old part of the city.

3 David is returning home ...
A tomorrow.
B in five days.
C next week.

2 Read the postcard again and match each paragraph with a statement. There is one statement you do not need to use.

1 Paragraph 1 says what David ___
2 Paragraph 2 says what David ___
3 Paragraph 3 says what David ___

a is doing for the next few days.
b is doing today and tomorrow.
c did yesterday and will do today.
d wants to know about Stan.

6

Doing it Right!

Reading

1 ➲ KET Read the article and for each question, choose the correct answer, A, B or C.

School at home? Yes!

Have you ever heard of school at home? No, we don't mean doing your homework at home – we mean having all your lessons at home! Every day in Australia, hundreds of children have school in their home! Why? Well, to answer this question you should look at the map of Australia. It's very big! Most people in Australia live in towns and cities next to the sea, but there are also some people who live in the middle of the country. The middle of Australia is called the 'outback'. It's very big and very hot. In the outback, families often live very far from each other. Many children live hundreds of miles from any primary or secondary school! They can't catch the bus or walk to school. School children in the outback often have to use the internet to study. These pupils have lessons every day. They stay at home and they go online!

Children who have school on the internet must study the same subjects as other pupils in Australia but of course they don't have to wear a uniform! They mustn't forget to do their homework every day – just like other pupils.

Every year, the students from the outback meet each other. Three or four times a year, for one week, the home-school pupils travel for many hours to spend time with their teachers and classmates. Peter is a student who studies online. What advice does he have for home-school pupils? 'That's easy! You should have a very good computer! Thanks to your computer you can stay in touch with your teachers and your friends. It's very, very important!'

1 All children in Australia have school at home.
A Right
B Wrong
C Doesn't say

2 Children in the outback often live very far from a school.
A Right
B Wrong
C Doesn't say

3 The pupils who have school online must study the same subjects as other children in Australia.
A Right
B Wrong
C Doesn't say

4 Children in the outback feel very lonely.
A Right
B Wrong
C Doesn't say

5 Some parents are not happy with the lessons on the internet.
A Right
B Wrong
C Doesn't say

6 Peter thinks that home-school pupils must have a good computer.
A Right
B Wrong
C Doesn't say

Wordpower!

2 Write a word from the box in each gap to complete the sentences.

group • interests • lonely • make • nervous • primary • secondary • touch

1 Harry doesn't have many friends. He often feels ________ .
2 My main ________ are basketball and music.
3 What a nice ________ of friends you have! They're great to hang out with.
4 'Do you get ________ before exams?' 'Yes, just a little.'
5 In my country children start ________ school when they are six years old.
6 You always ________ friends so quickly! It's amazing.
7 'How do you stay in ________ with all your friends?' 'I use the internet!'
8 My older brother is 16 and we go to the same ________ school.

3 Read the conversation and choose the correct word.

Kate: Dad, did you enjoy (1) **primary / uniform** school when you were young?

Dad: Yes, I loved it. I can still remember my teachers! I had great friends and I never felt (2) **lonely / secondary**. But then, when I was about 12 years old, we moved to a new area and I went to a big (3) **rule / secondary** school.

Kate: Did you (4) **make / interests** new friends quickly?

Dad: No, it was hard for me at first. I felt (5) **nervous / subjects** when I met new people. But I decided to join the basketball team. That was a very good idea.

Kate: Why?

Dad: Well, I met kids who had the same (6) **interests / rules** as me. It was fun and I had a new (7) **term / group** of friends to hang out with. You won't believe it, but I am still in (8) **make / touch** with them today.

Kate: Wow, that's amazing!

4 Complete the sentences with the correct word. The first letter is given to help you.

1 Do you have a special **i**________ or hobby?
2 I like your **g**________ of friends very much.
3 I will be 18 when I finish **s**________ .
4 Please stay in **t**________ when you move to another city.
5 Jane's got lots of friends. She's never **l**________ .
6 I'm sure that I'll **m**________ friends at my new school next year.
7 I didn't feel **n**________ before my exam today! I felt great.
8 I started **p**________ school when I was five years old.

Grammar 1

Modals 1: ability, permission, obligation and advice

Look again at *Grammar database 11* on page 150 before doing these exercises.

1 KET Read the email and for each question, choose the correct answer, A, B or C.

write reply send

To: Tanyacoolperson@tanya.com
Subject: My new school

Hi, Tanya,

How are you? Well, good news! My new school is amazing, I love it. I've already made good friends. Guess what – I (1) ___ wear a uniform! Well, except when we do sports. When we do sports we (2) ___ wear sports clothes, but that's fine. And I am so happy because our new house is next to the school and my little brother Tim and I (3) ___ walk to school! We (4) ___ take the bus! Unfortunately, Tim isn't very happy. I told him that he (5) ___ be nervous about meeting new people, but I think he feels lonely. Mum thinks he (6) ___ join a club so he (7) ___ meet people with the same interests as him. Anyway, I've got SO much homework tonight, so I (8) ___ stop here. Please tell me all your news.

Bye for now,

Paul

	A	B	C
1	A don't have to	B should	C must
2	A should	B have to	C can
3	A can	B should	C must
4	A mustn't	B can't	C don't have to
5	A shouldn't	B hasn't	C don't have to
6	A doesn't have to	B has	C should
7	A must	B can	C has to
8	A must	B could	C can

2 Write short answers.

1 Should I ask my teacher about the homework?
Yes, ________________ .

2 Do you have to wear a uniform to school?
No, ________________ .

3 Could I ask you a question, please?
Yes, ________________ .

4 Does your mother have to meet your teacher today?
Yes, ________________ .

5 Can I leave the class early today?
Yes, ________________ .

6 Does your brother have to go home now?
No, ________________ .

7 Do you have to study tonight?
Yes, ________________ .

8 Should I ask my dad for help?
No, ________________ .

3 Read the sentences and choose the option, a or b, which has the same meaning.

1 My little brother mustn't walk to school on his own. He's only six years old.
- **a** He shouldn't walk to school on his own, but he can if he wants to.
- **b** He is not allowed to walk to school on his own.

2 We don't have to finish our English project tonight.
- **a** It is not necessary to finish the project tonight, but you can if you want to.
- **b** You are not allowed to finish the project tonight.

3 You mustn't eat food during the lesson.
- **a** You can eat food during the lesson if you want to, but it is not necessary.
- **b** You are not allowed to eat food during the lesson.

4 I have to study tonight because we have an important history test tomorrow.
- **a** It is not necessary to study tonight, but I can if I want to.
- **b** I must study tonight.

Wordpower!

1 Write a word from the box in each gap to complete the sentences.

about • at • for • on • to • with

1 I'm sorry but I can't go to the party __________ you today.
2 My mum punished me __________ spilling all the drinks on the floor.
3 What did you learn __________ in the music lesson today?
4 My brother never listens __________ me when I talk to him!
5 I played basketball with my group of friends __________ school today.
6 My parents haven't decided __________ the best primary school for my little sister yet.

2 Match to make sentences.

1 Can you please listen ___
2 I learned ___
3 Thank you ___
4 The teacher didn't punish Fred ___
5 Have you decided ___
6 Do you always agree ___

a for breaking the window.
b for helping me!
c about places in London today.
d on a film?
e with your friends?
f to your teacher?

Listening

6

1 KET Julia is talking to her friend Adam about her new school. Listen and for each question, choose the correct answer, A, B or C.

1 How does Julia get to school?
A She takes a bus.
B She walks.
C Her mum drives her.

2 When she travels to school, ...
A she mustn't talk.
B she mustn't eat.
C she mustn't listen to music.

3 If you have a mobile phone, ...
A you can take it to school.
B you must give it to the teacher.
C you can use it in the lesson.

4 Julia must wear a school uniform ...
A every day.
B on school trips.
C when she plays sports with other schools.

5 When a teacher enters the class, the pupils have to ...
A say hello.
B stand up.
C sit down.

6 On Fridays, Julia can ...
A hang out with her new friends.
B go home early.
C join an interesting club.

Grammar 2 G

Modals 2: possibility and probability

Look again at *Grammar database 12* on page 150 before doing these exercises.

1 Put the words into the correct order to make sentences.

1 famous / day. / one / could / You / very / be ______
2 join / I / year. / the / video / might / club / this ______
3 should / This / good. / be / very / film ______
4 tomorrow. / test / We / have / a / might / maths ______
5 I / tomorrow. / may / for / school / late / be ______
6 may / It / today. / later / rain ______

2 Two friends are talking about joining a club. Read the conversation and for each question, choose the correct answer, A, B or C.

Jack: I haven't decided yet what club to join this year. I (1) ___ join the photography club. What do you think?

Sam: You're a really good guitarist. I think you (2) ___ join the music club. I'm sure you (3) ___ meet other musicians in that club. Hey! Maybe you could start a band!

Jack: That's a good idea!

Sam: I (4) ___ help you! I (5) ___ organise concerts for you! First, we (6) ___ think of a really good name for this new band – that's very important. How about 'The Cool Kids'? People (7) ___ like that name.

Jack: No, I don't like it!

Sam: Well, let's ask the other people in the band. They (8) ___ have some better ideas!

Jack: I hope so! OK, I (9) ___ go – see you later.

Sam: Bye … rock star of the future! Hey, one day you (10) ___ be really famous! Hahaha!

	A	B	C
1	**A** might	**B** have to	**C** will
2	**A** can	**B** should	**C** may
3	**A** must	**B** have to	**C** will
4	**A** could	**B** must	**C** should
5	**A** have to	**B** will	**C** might
6	**A** must	**B** may	**C** might
7	**A** can	**B** might	**C** have to
8	**A** must	**B** can	**C** may
9	**A** might	**B** have to	**C** can
10	**A** might	**B** should	**C** must

✔ Quick check

3 Put a line through the incorrect sentence.

1 You should to do all your homework. / You should do all your homework.
2 I not have to go to school today. / I don't have to go to school today.
3 You shouldn't be nervous. / You shouldn't being nervous.
4 I might to have an exam today. / I might have an exam today.
5 Our teacher may be away today. / Our teacher may to be away today.

Writing

You can give advice in two ways:

These are friendly ways to give advice.
You should write about your town.
How about writing about your school?
Why don't you write about your friends?
What about writing about your family?

These sentences are not very friendly.
You must write about your town!
Write about your friends!

1 Read the sentences and say if they are friendly (F) or not friendly (NF) ways to give advice.

1 How about studying with a friend at the weekend? F
2 Listen more carefully in the class! ___
3 You should join a club at school. ___
4 Make new friends! ___

2 Read this letter from John to his friend Ronnie and for each question, choose the correct answer.

1 Ronnie sent John an email about one week ago. **true / false**
2 John gives Ronnie friendly advice about the school project. **true / false**
3 John thinks the project is boring. **true / false**
4 How many main ideas does John suggest? **three / four / five**
5 What is John's first idea about? **rules / friends / classmates**
6 John suggests a second idea. What is it about? **music / hobbies / rules**
7 What is John's last suggestion about? **photos / teachers / buildings**
8 John uses this sentence: *Let me know if you need any more help*. Is this ...? **friendly / not friendly**

Dear Ronnie,

How are you? Thanks for your email last week. It was great to hear from you. I'm pleased that you are enjoying your new school and that you have made some new friends.

The project you described in your letter sounds very interesting! I have some ideas that might help you. The title of the project is 'Ways to Make my School Better' – is that right? Well first of all, how about talking about the rules? Are there any rules that the students would like to change? Have you spoken to your classmates about any of the rules that they don't like? Why don't you suggest some new rules?

I've got a second idea for your project too. How about talking about the clubs at the school? You might have some nice ideas about new hobbies for the pupils. Is there a music club or a film-making club? Why don't you suggest some new clubs that are interesting for people your age?

The third idea I had was about the buildings in the school. Why don't you suggest ways to make the buildings look nicer? How about some pictures or photos on the walls inside the school? That can make the classrooms look good. Do you think the teachers would like that idea?

Anyway, I hope these ideas are helpful. I look forward to reading your project. Send it to me by email when you have finished it. Let me know if you need any more help.

Bye for now,

John

Check your progress! | Units 5–6

1 Read the text and for each question, choose the correct answer, A, B or C.

School life is different for everyone. For some people, it's easy to (1) ___ friends, but others feel (2) ___ around their classmates. Some students really enjoy school. Others don't listen (3) ___ their teachers and they miss things.
It's important, though, to have a good (4) ___ of friends at school. Many students have got the same (5) ___, such as in music, sport, and films. Teachers can make school life fun also. They can (6) ___ things to do for their students. They can go on a school (7) ___ to an exciting place and learn (8) ___ history or science. They can also go on a guided (9) ___ of a museum or a castle.
One thing is true – school life can be an exciting (10) ___. Everyone can agree (11) ___ that!

	A	B	C
1	**A** get	**B** make	**C** do
2	**A** friendly	**B** happy	**C** nervous
3	**A** through	**B** at	**C** to
4	**A** club	**B** team	**C** group
5	**A** interests	**B** subjects	**C** terms
6	**A** organise	**B** find out	**C** visit
7	**A** tour	**B** guide	**C** trip
8	**A** at	**B** on	**C** about
9	**A** ticket	**B** tour	**C** book
10	**A** interest	**B** experience	**C** view
11	**A** with	**B** from	**C** for

11 marks

2 Write a word in each gap to complete the text.

For today's trip, we're (12) ________ to visit the London Eye first. The bus (13) ________ leaving in a few minutes, so everyone should be ready to go. I think we (14) ________ need our coats today, as it's a bit cold. Also, the sky isn't very clear, so we (15) ________ be able to see far, but it will (16) ________ fun to go on the ride. After the London Eye, we (17) ________ having lunch at *PizzaExpress* and then on to the British Museum.

6 marks

3 Choose the correct word or phrase.

18 The rules say we **have to / should** wear uniforms to school.
19 You **mustn't / don't have to** be late for your lessons.
20 Lisa **should / has to** join the basketball team if she likes basketball.
21 You **can / must** go to Laura's house to study if you want.
22 We **will / might** have a test in class tomorrow, but we're not sure.
23 Let me see if I **can / might** help you with your homework.
24 The school decided that we **may not / won't** have a party this year.
25 Mr Moore, **could / should** I ask you a question?

8 marks

Total: ___ / 25 marks

7

Make it, Build it!

Reading

1 ➲ KET Read the texts and for each question, choose the correct answer A, B or C.

Table tennis is quite a popular game these days. Like all games, it was invented by someone, but with this game, we're not sure who it was. It was first played in the 1880s by British people after their evening dinner. The dinner table was cleared and some books were stood up across the centre. The players used other books to hit a small ball across the table and over the books that were standing up. That's how table tennis was started!

1 Where was table tennis first played?

A in a sports centre
B in someone's home
C in a restaurant

The Mona Lisa is a painting that is known by many people. In this painting, a woman is shown sitting with her arms folded and smiling. It seems normal, doesn't it? However, it's her smile that makes this painting famous. The smile is very small and when you see it, you think, 'What is this woman thinking about?' It was painted in the 16th century by a man named Leonardo da Vinci, and it wasn't known who the woman in the painting was until 2005.

2 The Mona Lisa ...

A was painted in 2005.
B was painted by a woman.
C is a painting of a woman.

What building in Australia is known by most people in the world? If you say the Sydney Opera House, you're right. The building is known for its white top, which looks like a group of sailing boats sitting in the water. Music is played there, but the building is also used as a theatre, where plays are performed. It was designed by Danish architect Jorn Utzon in 1957, but the building wasn't completed until 1973.

3 The Sydney Opera House ...

A is used for music only.
B was designed in 1957.
C was built by a Danish man.

Today, the ancient Italian city of Pompeii is visited by millions of people every year. What makes this place so special? It was destroyed in 79 AD by the volcano that the city was built on. The city was completely covered and no one knew it was there for almost 1,700 years. Then, in 1749, the city's buildings were found in the ground. Scientists started to study the area to learn what life was like so many years ago, and many people visit it today for the same reasons.

4 Pompeii was covered in the ground ...

A for millions of years.
B for more than 1,700 years.
C for almost 1,700 years.

Many Americans believe that their country was discovered in 1492 by a man from Italy known as Christopher Columbus. This is true in a way, but Columbus never actually saw what is called the United States of America today. The first piece of land that he saw was an island known as Hispaniola, which is found hundreds of kilometres to the south-east of Miami. He made four trips from Spain to this island and other islands nearby, in Central America and South America, but he never reached North America.

5 The land that Christopher Columbus first saw is known as ...

A North America.
B Central America.
C Hispaniola.

Wordpower!

2 Each of the words in bold is in the wrong sentence. Write a word in bold from another sentence to replace the incorrect one.

1 Frank uses a **genius** in maths class. ____________
2 Can I use your **tower** phone to make a call? ____________
3 Lisa really enjoys living in a big **battery**. ____________
4 Rachel is a **calculator** at maths and gets very high marks. ____________
5 John's phone isn't working because the **mobile** is dead. ____________
6 You can see the whole town from this tall **city**. ____________

3 ➲ KET For each question, choose the correct word, A, B or C.

1 My cousin lives in the ___ of Manchester.
A cube **B** tower **C** city

2 He lives near a ___ that's got many floors.
A mobile **B** cube **C** tower

3 We're good friends and we talk on our ___ phones a lot.
A mobile **B** battery **C** calculator

4 We talked for two hours once and the ___ in my phone died.
A calculator **B** mobile **C** battery

5 He is a ___ at many things such as maths.
A cube **B** genius **C** tower

6 He hardly ever uses a ___ when he does his homework.
A tower **B** calculator **C** cube

7 He can ___ out the answer to a maths problem quickly.
A find **B** make **C** get

8 He's even got smart toys, such as a Rubik's ___ .
A phone **B** cube **C** tower

4 Write a word from the box in each gap.

battery • built • calculator • cities • designed found • genius • invented • towers

The first mobile phone was (1) __________ in 1973 by a man named Martin Cooper, who was a(n) (2) __________ with electronic devices. He (3) __________ the first mobile phone to look like a phone, but it didn't look like the ones we use today. It was a very large, heavy phone, and the (4) __________ only lasted for 20 minutes. However, Cooper said that wasn't a problem because 'you couldn't hold the phone up for that long.' Since then, people have (5) __________ out ways to make mobile phones very small. They can also be used for other things, like planning your day, or as a(n) (6) __________ to do simple maths problems. They are used in both big (7) __________ and small towns. They can be used in the countryside too, thanks to tall (8) __________ that mobile phone companies have (9) __________ . Mobile phones have become so important that most of us couldn't live without them.

Grammar 1 G

The passive 1

Look again at *Grammar database 13* on page 150 before doing these exercises.

1 Choose the correct word or phrase.

1 Tower Bridge **was / were** completed in 1894.
2 Batteries **was / were** invented in 1800 by Alessandro Volta.
3 In what year was **discovered Pompeii / Pompeii discovered**?
4 The Eiffel Tower **is / are** visited by many people each year.
5 Refrigerators **are / aren't** used to keep food cold.
6 **Is / Are** the digital camera often used in photography?

2 Put the verbs into the passive to complete the sentences.

1 This photo of the Empire State Building ______________ (**take**) in 2001.
2 Some stones in Stonehenge ______________ (**carry**) for 250 kilometres.
3 These buildings ______________ (**build**) over 2,000 years ago.
4 These days, car parks ______________ (**find**) in every big city.
5 Your kitchen is very clean. ______________ it ______________ (**clean**) every night?
6 This laptop ______________ (**not buy**) in the USA. I bought it in London.

3 Write a word from the box in each gap.

are • is • isn't • was • wasn't • weren't

The mobile phone has been around since the 1970s, but the idea behind the text message (1) __________ developed until the 1980s. Then, years later, the first text message (2) __________ sent in the UK in 1992. When people started to use mobile phones, text messages (3) __________ used very often. Now, millions of text messages (4) __________ sent every day. Information (5) __________ written by using the numbers on the phone to make words. People like text messages because they're cheap. So, a lot of money (6) __________ spent to send them.

4 ➲ KET Write a word in each gap to complete the text.

A lot of work in the office (1) __________ done on laptops. This is because laptops (2) __________ easily carried from the office to the home. Of course, the laptop of today (3) __________ made to be easy to pick up and carry. However, the first laptops (4) __________ designed in that way. The first laptop (5) __________ built in 1975 and it was very heavy. In fact, it was the same size as today's regular computer, and it (6) __________ used by many people at all.

Wordpower!

1 KET Write a phrase for each description. The first letter of each word is given to help you.

1 This is where you can buy stamps. **p** ___ ___ ___ **o** ___ ___ ___ ___ ___
2 This is where many important things happen in a town.
t ___ ___ ___ **h** ___ ___ ___
3 You put clothes in this to clean them.
w ___ ___ ___ ___ ___ ___ **m** ___ ___ ___ ___ ___ ___
4 This is used to cook food. **m** ___ ___ ___ ___ ___ ___ ___ ___ **o** ___ ___ ___
5 This tells you what time it is. **d** ___ ___ ___ ___ ___ ___ **c** ___ ___ ___ ___
6 This is used to play music. **M** ___ ___ **p** ___ ___ ___ ___ ___
7 This is where many people work. **o** ___ ___ ___ ___ ___ **b** ___ ___ ___ ___
8 Paintings are kept here. **a** ___ ___ **g** ___ ___ ___ ___ ___ ___

2 Match to make sentences.

1 You can use my mobile ___
2 Lisa leaves her car in the car ___
3 I like the shopping ___
4 The clothes in the washing ___
5 Mike works at a police ___
6 The food in the microwave ___
7 My MP3 ___
8 Fred works in an art ___

a station in the city centre.
b centre on Riley Avenue.
c gallery on Taylor Street.
d oven is very hot.
e phone to make a call.
f player's got 700 songs.
g machine aren't clean.
h park across the street.

Listening

7

1 Listen to the speaker talking about music players and write a word or number to complete the sentences.

1 The MP3 player is used by both young people and ________ .
2 The *Listen Up* MP3 player was created in ________ .
3 Only ________ of the *Listen Up* MP3 players were made.
4 The *MPMan* was sold in the ________ .
5 The *Rio PMP300* could play music for up to ________ hour(s).

Grammar 2

The passive 2: using *by*

Look again at *Grammar database 14* on page 151 before doing these exercises.

1 KET Read the text and for each question, choose the correct word, A, B or C to complete the text.

The photograph (1) ___ invented almost two hundred years ago (2) ___ 1824 (3) ___ a man named Joseph Nicéphore Niépce. The camera he used to make the photograph (4) ___ made of wood. The first colour photograph (5) ___ taken (6) ___ a man named James Clerk Maxwell (7) ___ 1861. Both men created other things in life, but they (8) ___ remembered today (9) ___ most people for these first photographs.

	A	B	C
1	**A** is	**B** was	**C** were
2	**A** in	**B** by	**C** with
3	**A** to	**B** in	**C** by
4	**A** was	**B** were	**C** is
5	**A** is	**B** was	**C** were
6	**A** by	**B** in	**C** from
7	**A** in	**B** at	**C** by
8	**A** is	**B** were	**C** are
9	**A** by	**B** in	**C** with

2 Write sentences in the passive using *in*.

1 the White House / finish / 1800 ____________________
2 telephones / invent / 1876 ____________________
3 The first DVD / sell / 1996 ____________________
4 paper / develop / the year 105 ____________________

3 Rewrite the sentences in the passive using *by*.

1 The Egyptians built the pyramids. ____________________
2 A Frenchman designed the Statue of Liberty. ____________________
3 Nintendo makes terrific games consoles. ____________________
4 Young people often use the MP3 player. ____________________
5 A terrible storm destroyed the old house. ____________________
6 Millions of people visit the Great Wall of China. ____________________

Quick check

4 Choose the correct answer.

1 Do we use the passive when it's important who does something? **yes / no**
2 Do we use the past participle of the main verb in a passive sentence? **yes / no**
3 Which is correct? **Computers are made here. / Computers made here. / both**
4 Do we use *in* after the passive to say who does or did something? **yes / no**
5 Do we use *by* when we don't know who does or did something? **yes / no**
6 Which is correct? **These were made by Joe. / These were made in 1991. / both**

Writing

A **Bring The Sky Into Your Bedroom!**

B

C **Is it hard to go to sleep at night? Do you have to wake up really early in the morning, even before the sun comes up? With the amazing new Sky Clock, your troubles may soon be over! Here are a few of the fantastic things the Sky Clock will do for you!**

D
- The Sky Clock is like the sun in the morning. When the alarm goes off, the Sky Clock turns into the sun! Light is shone through the clock's face. It's brilliant!
- The Sky Clock is like a bird in the morning. Bird sounds are heard coming from the clock's speaker. Say goodbye to those terrible sounds that are made by other alarm clocks!
- The Sky Clock is like the night sky at night. Stars are shown on the walls of your bedroom, and they're turned off when you're sleeping. It's really cool!

E *The Sky Clock is loved by everyone who buys it.*
It's sold in shops all across the country.

F **Get yours today!**

1 **Read the advert and choose the correct word or phrase.**

1 The Sky Clock is for your **living room / bedroom**.
2 The Sky Clock is good for people who **hate the sun / can't sleep at night**.
3 The Sky Clock uses light from **the sun / inside the clock** to shine light in the room.
4 When the Sky Clock's alarm goes off, the Sky Clock makes **bird sounds / a terrible sound**.
5 At night, the Sky Clock shows **the sun / stars** on your wall.
6 The Sky Clock is sold in **many countries / many shops**.

2 **Read the advert again and match each part with a statement.**

1 Part A is ___	**a** what the item can do.
2 Part B shows ___	**b** what the item looks like.
3 Part C describes ___	**c** what to do next.
4 Part D lists ___	**d** the title of the advert.
5 Part E tells us ___	**e** where you can buy the item.
6 Part F tells us ___	**f** who the item is for.

8

Weird World!

Reading

1 ➲ KET Read the five texts and match them to the sentences (a–e).

a The project is about different animals.
b We had to stay inside.
c I need advice about my pet.
d There will be more earthquakes.
e A teenager has just won something.

1 ___

write reply send

Hi, Tony,

How are you? Can you help me? Last night there was a really scary thunderstorm in our area. All night there were flashes of lightning and then the sound of thunder. My problem was my little dog. He was so frightened! Every time he heard the thunder, he ran under my bed. I felt very sorry for him. Does your dog usually get frightened, too? What do you think I should do when this happens again?

Jack

2 ___

Another Earthquake!

Last night at 3.57 in the morning another earthquake was recorded. Fortunately, nobody was hurt, but the bridge over the river was destroyed. There have already been three earthquakes in two months and scientists say that there will probably be more. Everybody should be very careful, especially families with small children.

3 ___

THE WINNER ★

Hey, Kids! This week the prize goes to fourteen-year-old Jamie Maxwell from Kingston! Jamie sent us a weird story about things falling from the sky – and this is a TRUE story! Did you know that it can rain fish? And how about frogs? Yes! Winds can pick up these very small creatures from the sea or the ground and carry them thousands of miles to other countries. Jamie says that these winds even carried little frogs from Africa across the sea to Spain! Jamie, an iPod™ is your prize for this amazing story!

4 ___

write reply send

Hey, Anna,

Did you feel the earthquake last night? I thought mum was shaking me to wake me up, but it wasn't her – the ground was shaking. SCARY. All the pictures on my wall fell down! Your house is near mine, so I guess you woke up too. What did you do? I wanted to go outside, but Dad said we shouldn't do that. Anyway, we all stayed under the big table in our living room for about an hour. Do you know if the school is open today? Call me when you read this.

Mike

5 ___

Pupils in group A must write about creatures that we find in the desert. Write about how they live and what they eat. How do they live in such high temperatures?

Pupils in group B, you must write about the lake near our town. What creatures live there and where do they go when the temperature falls and the lake turns to ice? How do these animals find food in the ice?

Please have this project ready for Monday morning to show the class.

Wordpower!

2 Write a word from the box in each gap to complete the sentences.

common • creatures • flash • ground • lake • temperature • thunderstorm • weird

1 Does the ________ ever reach 40°C in your country?
2 Every summer we swim in the ________ near our town.
3 Did you see that ________ of lightning? It was amazing!
4 My glasses fell on the ________ and I can't find them now!
5 Are earthquakes ________ in your country?
6 What's that ________ noise? It sounds like a cat crying!
7 You shouldn't go swimming when there's a ________. It can be very dangerous.
8 I think frogs are very strange little ________.

3 Complete the sentences with the correct word. The first letter is given to help you.

1 Have you ever seen a **f**________ of lightning?
2 I can't remember the name of the **l**________ in your area. Can you swim in it?
3 Wow! Listen to the noise of that **t**________. Amazing!
4 In winter the **t**________ falls and there is snow everywhere.
5 Don't you think the whale is an amazing **c**________?
6 During the earthquake the **g**________ opened up right in front of me!
7 That's **w**________! I'm sure I closed the window – but now it's open again.
8 Are thunderstorms **c**________ in your country?

4 Match to make sentences.

1 That flash of ___
2 What temperature does it ___
3 I think that penguins ___
4 Are storms ___
5 What's that weird ___
6 In this game, the ball mustn't ___
7 Can you catch fish ___
8 Listen to the sound ___

a in the lake?
b of that thunder!
c hit the ground.
d fall to in winter?
e lightning was so close to us!
f animal sitting in the garden?
g are funny creatures.
h common here in summer?

Grammar 1

Articles 1

Look again at *Grammar database 15* on page 151 before doing these exercises.

1 Choose the correct word. A dash (–) means no article is necessary.

1 Have you ever felt **an / a** earthquake?
2 Would you like to travel to **the / an** USA?
3 **The / A** River Nile is in Egypt.
4 I saw an amazing film about **the** / – Mount Everest.
5 **The** / – strong winds last night destroyed some small trees in our garden.
6 Have you ever been very close to **a / the** flash of lightning?
7 **The** / – Italy is a country I would love to visit.
8 Wow, look at **a / the** sky! It's red and orange!

2 Two friends, Rob and Emma, are talking about places they would like to visit. Read the conversation and for each question, choose the correct answer, A, B or C. A dash (–) means no article is necessary.

Rob: Emma, what country would you like to visit?
Emma: Oh, that's (1) ___ easy question! I'd like to go to (2) ___ New Zealand.
Rob: New Zealand? Where's that?
Emma: It's (3) ___ small country in (4) ___ Pacific Ocean.
Rob: Oh, of course! It's near (5) ___ Antarctic.
Emma: Yes, that's right. But (6) ___ weather in New Zealand is much warmer! In summer, (7) ___ temperatures can reach 35° to 40°C!
Rob: That's hot! I've heard that it's (8) ___ very beautiful country.
Emma: Yes, a lot of films are made there because (9) ___ mountains and the forests are so amazing.
Rob: I think there was (10) ___ very bad earthquake there last month.
Emma: Yes, that's right. Unfortunately, (11) ___ earthquakes are common in New Zealand.
Rob: Oh, dear. I hope that (12) ___ people in that area are OK.

	A	B	C
1	**A** –	**B** a	**C** an
2	**A** the	**B** a	**C** –
3	**A** a	**B** the	**C** an
4	**A** –	**B** the	**C** a
5	**A** the	**B** an	**C** –
6	**A** the	**B** –	**C** a
7	**A** an	**B** a	**C** the
8	**A** a	**B** the	**C** –
9	**A** the	**B** an	**C** a
10	**A** an	**B** the	**C** a
11	**A** the	**B** –	**C** an
12	**A** the	**B** a	**C** an

3 Read the sentences and choose the correct answer, a or b.

1 Do you know how many different creatures live on **the** Earth? — We use *the* in this sentence because ...
a the Earth is a noun.
b there is only one Earth.

2 **The** big green frog you saw yesterday isn't dangerous. — We use *the* because ...
a we are talking about a specific frog.
b frogs are nouns.

3 Have you ever seen **the** Amazon River? — We use *the* in this sentence because ...
a we are talking about a specific noun.
b we usually use *the* with names of rivers.

4 I hope I can go to London one day! — There is **no article** before *London* because ...
a we generally do not use an article before place names.
b there is only one city called London.

Wordpower!

1 **Complete the sentences with the correct form of the word in bold**

1 My hat blew into the trees because the weather was so __________ . **wind**
2 What a lovely __________ day! Let's go for a walk. **sun**
3 In winter, __________ weather in the mountains is common. **mist**
4 I can't see the mountains because it's so __________ . **fog**
5 I love __________ weather. **snow**
6 In __________ weather there's ice on the ground and on the trees. **frost**
7 I won't take a picture now – it's too __________ . **cloud**
8 I usually enjoy travelling by plane, but not in __________ weather! **storm**
9 'Is it true that the weather in England is __________ ?' 'Yes, very true!' **rain**

2 **Choose the correct word.**

1 Be careful! You shouldn't stay in the **sunny / sun** for a long time.
2 I think my favourite weather is when it's **mist / misty**. The trees look so nice then!
3 Look at the sky! I think a **storm / stormy** is coming.
4 We couldn't see other people in the park because it was very **fog / foggy**.
5 It's very **rain / rainy** today. I don't want to play basketball outside.
6 Oh, dear! Look at that big black **cloud / cloudy**. I think it's going to rain.
7 'Do you like **snow / snowy** weather?' 'No, I don't like cold weather at all!'
8 I love walking in the park when it's **wind / windy**.
9 Look at the **frost / frosty** on the ground. It looks like ice!

Listening

8

1 **Listen to four short conversations.**
For each conversation, choose the true statement, A, B or C.

1 **A** The girl took an amazing photograph.
B The photograph is black and white.
C They both like the photograph.

2 **A** Frogs are common in the city.
B Frogs live near the lake.
C The girl doesn't like frogs.

3 **A** Peter felt an earthquake.
B Peter's family was hurt.
C Peter broke a window.

4 **A** Tim is writing a book about storms.
B The book is about dangerous films.
C The book is about people making films.

8

2 **Listen again and decide if the statements are true (T) or false (F).**

1 In Dialogue 1, the girl likes the colours in the photo. T/F
2 In Dialogue 2, the girl often sees frogs where she lives. T/F
3 In Dialogue 3, the books in Peter's class fell on the ground. T/F
4 In Dialogue 4, the people in Tim's book have never been hit by lightning. T/F

Grammar 2

G

Countable and uncountable nouns 1

Look again at *Grammar database 16* on page 151 before doing these exercises.

1 Look at these countable and uncountable nouns. Write C for countable noun or UC for uncountable noun.

1 knowledge ___
2 water ___
3 animal ___
4 advice ___
5 idea ___
6 air ___
7 desert ___
8 creature ___
9 river ___
10 help ___
11 information ___
12 storm ___

2 Read Christine's email to her friend and for each question, choose the correct answer. A dash (–) means no article is necessary.

write reply send

To: David Bale <dave.protectanimals@fastmail.com>
Subject: Help with my project

Hey, Dave,

How are things? I know you love (1) **the / -** animals. Can you help me? I am doing (2) **the / a** project for my school and I need (3) **the / some** help. Can you please send me (4) **some / an** information about penguins and different creatures that live in (5) **a / the** snow. How do these animals stay warm? Do they have a lot of (6) **the / -** hair so they are warm in winter? I saw on the internet that (7) **the / an** animals that live in cold places sometimes sleep in winter. Is that true? Can you give me (8) **some / the** advice for this project please?

Bye for now,

Christine

✓ Quick check

3 Put a line through the incorrect sentence.

1 Do you like the little lake in our town? /
Do you like little lake in our town?
2 I don't like earthquakes! /
I don't like the earthquakes!
3 Frogs in that river make weird noises. /
The frogs in that river make weird noises.
4 I think the information in this book about storms is wrong. /
I think information in this book about storms are wrong.
5 Have you ever seen lightning? /
Have you ever seen a lightning?

Writing

Use adjectives to make the title interesting.
'The fantastic mountains'
'A wonderful day'
'Frightening creatures on our planet'

1 Read the titles and say if there is an adjective (A) or if there isn't an adjective (NA).

1 'The forest' NA
2 'An exciting day in my life' ____
3 'An amazing creature' ____
4 'A lake' ____
5 'The thunderstorm' ____
6 'A scary night' ____

2 Underline the adjectives in these sentences.

1 This is an amazing place to visit.
2 People love having picnics in these beautiful mountains.
3 Many big trees are next to the lake.
4 This is a wonderful forest to walk in.

3 Read this description of a favourite local place and for each question, choose the correct answer, A, B or C.

A beautiful beach

(1) My town is very near the sea and my favourite local place is a lovely beach called Sandy Beach. Sandy Beach might sound like a strange name for a beach because all beaches have sand. But the sand at this beach is very special. It isn't brown or black sand – it's white, really white! People love taking photos of the beach because the sand looks so beautiful. Nobody knows when the beach got the name Sandy Beach, but it's been called that for years!

(2) Sandy Beach is a very long beach and in the summer the water is very blue. There are lots of very big trees and in the summer when the temperature rises and it's very hot, people sit under these trees. But in the winter when the weather is stormy, the beach can be very windy. Sometimes when it's foggy, you can hear ships in the sea but you can't see anything! It can be very exciting to walk along the beach in the winter when there's a storm, but it's very dangerous to swim in the sea!

(3) Sandy Beach is very popular in the summer because everyone, old people and young people, can have a nice time. There are so many nice things to do at this beach. Families often have picnics under the trees and children can play on the beach or build castles in the sand. And of course, people have fun swimming and playing in the sea. In the evening, it is common for groups of young people to hang out with their friends on the beach. Sometimes they bring their guitars and play music. I think Sandy Beach is wonderful!

1 Paragraph 1 talks about ...
A the local weather.
B the name of the beach.
C local photographers.

2 Paragraph 2 describes ...
A the beach in different seasons.
B ships in stormy weather.
C a forest near the beach.

3 In the winter, sometimes you can only hear ships because ...
A the sea is dangerous.
B there are many thunderstorms.
C there is fog.

4 Paragraph 3 describes ...
A the weather.
B things you can do at the beach.
C the sea.

Check your progress! | Units 7–8

1 **Read the conversation and for each question, choose the correct answer, A, B or C.**

Anna: Hey, Sam, where have you been? I tried calling your mobile (1) ___ before but it wasn't working. I think it might be broken.

Sam: No, it isn't broken. I have to buy a new (2) ___ for it, that's all. I'm going to that new shopping (3) ___ now. Do you want to come with me?

Anna: You mean the one next to the police (4) ___? Maybe that's not a good idea. It could be dangerous.

Sam: What are you talking about? Why might it be dangerous?

Anna: Haven't you heard the news? There is a very big (5) ___ coming. There might be (6) ___ of lightning and even (7) ___. You should stay at home!

Sam: Really? But, look, it's a beautiful (8) ___ day today. I can't see any black (9) ___ in the sky!

Anna: Well, I think you go home and stay inside!

Sam: OK, maybe you're right. Let's talk later. Bye.

1	**A** machine	**B** phone	**C** player
2	**A** battery	**B** digital	**C** clock
3	**A** office	**B** station	**C** centre
4	**A** station	**B** oven	**C** block
5	**A** thunderstorm	**B** temperature	**C** lightning
6	**A** frost	**B** ground	**C** flashes
7	**A** shower	**B** thunder	**C** earthquake
8	**A** sun	**B** sunny	**C** snow
9	**A** fog	**B** mist	**C** clouds

9 marks

2 **Put the verbs into the passive to complete the sentences.**

10 A famous old castle in London ________________ (**call**) the Tower of London.
11 My MP3 player ________________ (**give**) to me for my birthday.
12 Every year, new skyscrapers ________________ (**build**) in our city.
13 The old art gallery in our town ________________ (**design**) by a very famous person.
14 Unfortunately, many buildings ________________ (**destroy**) when the earthquake happened last month.
15 Stonehenge ________________ (**visit**) by thousands of people each year.
16 Oh, no! I think my mobile phone ________________ (**steal**)! It has disappeared!
17 When a thunderstorm is coming, people ________________ (**tell**) to stay indoors.
18 I think the first computers ________________ (**invent**) when my dad was a child!

9 marks

3 **Choose the correct answer. A dash (–) means no article is necessary.**

19 Wow! Look at this great photo of **the** / – Mount Everest.
20 One day I would love to visit **the / an** Antarctic.
21 Have you ever been to **the** / – Spain?
22 Don't look at **the / a** sun! It's not good for your eyes.
23 I used the internet to get **some / an** information about deserts around the world.
24 **The / A** lake in our town is a very nice place to visit.
25 I love **the** / – thunderstorms, but my little dog hates them.

7 marks

Total: ___ / 25 marks

9

Want any more?

Reading

1 ➲ KET Match each sign (A–G) to a statement. There is one sign you do not need to use.

1 You can't have a meal at this place. ____
2 This place has got cold meals only. ____
3 Meals at this place are cheap when you eat early. ____
4 This place has got one meal and it's not very healthy. ____
5 This is a good place for the morning. ____
6 You can get a burger with a salad here. ____

A

Al's Hamburgers
Great burgers and chips
That's all we make!

B

Sally's Salad Bar
Fresh, tasty and healthy
Only the best!

C

Rachel's Café
Sandwiches and burgers
Salads and more

D

THE COFFEE POT
Eggs with toast, fruit
Breakfast until 11am

E

PASTA ITALIANA
Over 20 pasta dishes
Half-price dinners before 6pm

F

PAUL'S Sandwich Shop
Hot and cold sandwiches
With chips or soup

G

Mel's SUPERMARKET
The best products in town

Wordpower!

2 KET Write a word or phase for each description. The first letter is given to help you.

1 When you use a knife to divide food into pieces, you do this. **c**__ __
2 You keep these kinds of food very, very cold. **f**__ __ __ __ __
3 This type of food is small and you have it between meals. **s**__ __ __ __
4 Drinks that have got bubbles are this. **f**__ __ __ __
5 When you cook something in hot oil, you do this. **f**__ __
6 This describes food that is nice. **t**__ __ __ __
7 The different things that you use to make a cake are these.
i__ __ __ __ __ __ __ __ __ __
8 Fruit and vegetables are examples of this type of food. **f**__ __ __ __
9 This is what you call food or drinks without sugar.
s__ __ __ __ **-f**__ __ __
10 This looks and tastes like butter. **m**__ __ __ __ __ __ __ __ __

3 Write a word or phrase from exercise 2 in each gap.

My mum doesn't like (1) ________ food, so our freezer hasn't got any food in it. She buys a lot of (2) ________ food like apples and oranges and different kinds of vegetables. We've got food in the fridge, of course, but it's all healthy. My mum doesn't (3) ________ food because she doesn't like all the oil. When we want something small to eat, we use a knife to (4) ________ a piece of fruit, and we have it as a(n) (5) ________ . When my mum cooks she uses healthy (6) ________ and she doesn't use a lot of sugar or butter. If she doesn't want to use butter, she'll use (7) ________ because it tastes the same and it's healthier. She's a really good cook, so all her food is (8) ________ . We love it! Oh, and one more thing. We haven't got any (9) ________ drinks in the house either. Those have got a lot of sugar. We've got drinks that are (10) ________ and they taste great without sugar!

Grammar 1

G

Countable and uncountable nouns 2

Look again at *Grammar database 17* on page 151 before doing these exercises.

1 Match to make sentences.

1	There are a few ___	**a**	cheese left in the packet.
2	Can you get a little ___	**b**	of coffee for the morning?
3	Are there a lot of ___	**c**	eggs in the fridge.
4	There are lots ___	**d**	bread on your way home?
5	There's not much ___	**e**	of apples in your kitchen.
6	Is there a lot ___	**f**	drinks for the party?

2 For each question, choose the correct word or phrase, A, B or C.

1 We haven't got ___ rice in the cupboard.
A a lot of
B many
C little

2 There's ___ orange juice left.
A not many
B not much
C a few

3 Can you buy a ___ potatoes on your way home?
A little
B lot
C few

4 There's ___ margarine left if you want it.
A a little
B lot of
C many

5 The restaurant's got ___ bottles of ketchup.
A a little
B many
C lots

6 Fizzy drinks have got ___ sugar in them.
A lots of
B many
C few

3 Write a word from the box in each gap.

few • little • lot • lots • many • much

Carol eats a lot of food that isn't very healthy. She loves cakes with a (1) ________ of sugar and butter in them. In her house, there are a (2) ________ vegetables and some fruit. But there are (3) ________ of packets of crisps in her cupboards. There are also (4) ________ fizzy drinks in the fridge – at least 20! There's just not (5) ________ healthy food in Carol's house. She's got a (6) ________ fresh food, but she should have more of it!

4 ➲ KET Write a word in each gap.

Mike and David eat very different things. Mike likes to eat healthy food. He doesn't like food with (1) ________ lot of fat in it. He eats lots (2) ________ fruit and vegetables and drinks sugar-free drinks. He doesn't like cheese, so there's (3) ________ much of it in his house. David, however, loves cheese, particularly on pizzas and pasta. He eats (4) ________ few bananas, but really, there's not a lot (5) ________ fruit in David's kitchen. And he won't have drinks without (6) ________ little sugar in them!

Wordpower!

1 Choose the correct word, A, B or C.

1 Lisa waited ___ the waiter to bring her lunch.
A like B of C for

2 My bacon and eggs look ___ a happy face!
A like B from C of

3 They left after they paid ___ their food.
A with B for C from

4 This meal tastes ___ ketchup.
A from B with C of

5 Eggs come ___ chickens.
A for B from C like

6 Margarine tastes ___ butter.
A with B from C like

7 Pasta doesn't go ___ sandwiches!
A with B like C for

8 Cheese is made ___ milk.
A for B to C from

2 Write a word from the box in each gap.

come • for • from • go • like • look • pay • taste

Crisps are a very popular snack. Most crisps are made (1) ________ potatoes. They are fried in oil and most of them (2) ________ like light brown or yellow circles after they're finished. They taste great, but they don't taste (3) ________ potatoes any more after they're cooked this way! They often (4) ________ of salt, since salt is added to them after they are cooked. They can (5) ________ from any place in the world, as every country makes its own kind of crisps. They're the perfect snack for when you're waiting (6) ________ someone and you want something quick to eat. They're cheap too. In most places, you usually only (7) ________ about €1 for a packet, maybe a little more. They (8) ________ well with sandwiches also, and that's another reason why they're so popular!

Listening

9

1 KET Listen to two teenagers talking about food and for each question, choose the correct word or phrase, A, B or C.

1 Which food does Jane see a lot of people eating?
A hamburgers
B fruit
C vegetables

2 Russell says many places make food ...
A that is fresh.
B very quickly.
C that is healthy.

3 Jane says fresh food ...
A is always healthy.
B is sometimes healthy.
C is never healthy.

4 The salad that Jane got in a restaurant the other day ...
A was very healthy.
B wasn't fresh.
C had a lot of oil.

5 What did Jane do with her salad?
A She ate it all.
B She didn't eat any of it.
C She ate a little of it.

6 How does Jane order salads now?
A with lots of oil
B with no oil
C with a little oil

Grammar 2

G

Clauses and connectives

Look again at *Grammar database 18* on page 151 before doing these exercises.

1 **Each of the words in bold is in the wrong sentence. Write a word in bold from another sentence to replace the incorrect one.**

1 That's the restaurant **and** we had pizza last night. ____________
2 I would like a sandwich **when** I would like some crisps to go with it. ____________
3 I tried to order the fish **or** they didn't have any left. ____________
4 I don't drink milk **where** I don't like the taste. ____________
5 Do you remember **but** we had coffee at that café? ____________
6 We can stay in **because** we can go out. Which do you prefer? ____________

2 **Complete the sentences with a word from the box.**

and • because • but • or • when • where

1 Julie likes oranges __________ they're tasty and healthy.
2 Martha loves fizzy drinks __________ she never drinks them.
3 I usually eat an apple __________ I want a snack.
4 This restaurant's got pizza __________ it's also got pasta.
5 This is the cupboard __________ we put tins of soup.
6 Do you want chicken __________ would you like hamburgers?

3 **Choose the correct word.**

Many people eat vegetarian food (1) **and / because** they don't like meat. They go to restaurants (2) **when / where** they've got only vegetarian meals on the menu. Vegetarian meals in restaurants are usually healthy (3) **and / or** they're often quite tasty too. A few items on a vegetarian menu are not very healthy (4) **or / because** they're made with a lot of oil. The recipe for the meal may contain a lot of oil (5) **but / or** the restaurant may put a lot of oil on after. So, people must choose carefully (6) **because / when** they are having a vegetarian dinner. Also, you can enjoy a great vegetarian meal (7) **where / when** you're cooking at home. You can get vegetarian recipes online (8) **or / where** you can buy a recipe book at a bookshop. You can practise cooking vegetarian meals you know (9) **or / but** you can try new recipes. You can have vegetarian dinner parties for friends (10) **when / and** you know how to cook many different recipes. The best thing is that you can choose recipes you like (11) **and / where** you can also decide how much oil to use!

Quick check

4 Choose the correct answer.

1 Do we use *many* with countable nouns? **yes / no**
2 Do we use *a few* with uncountable nouns? **yes / no**
3 Which is correct? **I eat lots of butter. / I eat lots of apples. / both**
4 Do we use *and* to talk about contrast? **yes / no**
5 Do we use *or* to talk about a choice? **yes / no**
6 Which is correct? **I like tomatoes but they're tasty. / I like tomatoes because they're tasty. / both**

Writing

1 Read this recipe and match each definition with a part of the recipe (A–F).

1 This tells us what food we need. ___
2 This gives us the instructions. ___
3 This tells us what other things we need. ___
4 This tells us the name of the recipe. ___
5 This gives us extra information. ___
6 This tells us how much time we need. ___

2 For each question, choose the correct answer A, B or C.

1 What is this recipe for?
A tomato sauce
B a hot pasta dish
C a fresh salad

2 How many vegetables are in the recipe?
A one
B two
C three

3 Where does the pasta go after it's cooked?
A in cold water
B in hot water
C in the bowl

4 Which ingredients may not be necessary?
A cheese
B tomatoes
C salt

A Fresh pasta salad

This is a great recipe for a nice cool pasta salad that's perfect to enjoy in the summer.

B Preparation time: 20 minutes

C **Ingredients:**

1 packet of pasta
3 large fresh tomatoes, cut into pieces
1 onion, cut into very small pieces
1 cup of cheese
3 tablespoons of oil
salt

D **You'll also need:**

1 large cooking pot filled with water
1 large bowl

E **What to do:**

- Cook the pasta in boiling hot water for 10 minutes.
- While the pasta is cooking, cut the tomatoes and onions into small pieces and put them in the bowl with the cheese.
- Put the pasta in very cold water when it is cooked.
- When the pasta is cold, take it out of the water and put it in the bowl with the tomatoes, onions and cheese.
- Use a spoon to stir the mixture for 2 minutes.
- You can add a little salt to the salad if you like.
- Your pasta salad is ready to eat!

F **Note:** This recipe makes enough pasta salad for two people. If you don't finish all of it, you can put it in a bowl and keep it in the fridge for three days.

10

All Sorts of People!

Reading

1 ➲ KET Read the six texts and match each text with one of the statements.

a I love children. In the mornings, I am busy.
b I love music and I enjoy meeting new people.
c I've got a lot of time in the mornings and I like to organise things.
d I like working with other people and I love painting.
e I am a shy person but I love computers.
f Everyone tells me that I look very good in photos.

1 ___

Do you love computers?

- Are you artistic?
- Do you like working on your own?
- Maybe this is the job for you! We need someone to help us with web design. Don't worry if you are a quite shy person – you do NOT have to work with a lot of people.
- We are a very small office but we're very friendly! Call us now for more information!

2 ___

Where are the beautiful people?

- We need beautiful people to be in a new film about FASHION!
- Do your friends tell you that you are a handsome guy?
- Do you love wearing trendy new clothes?
- Well, maybe you are the right person for us!
- Don't be shy! Call us NOW! Your life could change forever!

3 ___

Are you sociable? Do you like working with children? I need a cheerful, friendly person to help me at home with my two little children, ages two and five. Tuesday and Thursday afternoon from 3pm-6pm. Call Sandy on 2075557834.

4 ___

DO YOU LIKE MUSIC?

- Are you polite? Do you enjoy talking to new people?
- We are looking for someone to help us with our new music group. You must be friendly and good with people. We are musicians but we are NOT good organisers! Please help us find work so we can play at concerts in the small towns around! Call us now!

5 ___

Artists, actors and writers wanted now!!!

Can you make people laugh? Are you funny? Can you tell good jokes?

Are you artistic? Can you draw well? We are looking for people to help us with our new school play! It's very funny! Please join the theatre club and help us!

6 ___

The children in the town need you!

Do you have free time to help us? We need kind, generous people to organise the **big summer picnic** for the children in our town. This year, it will be at a beautiful lake in the mountains. We meet every Monday and Wednesday morning to organise everything. Come on! We need your help!

Wordpower!

2 Write a word in each gap to complete the sentences. The first letter is given to help you.

1 That new **g**________ in your basketball team is a very good player!
2 Don't be **s**________! Come and meet everyone!
3 Please don't talk when I'm speaking. It's not very **p**________.
4 You are very **a**________. These photos are amazing!
5 My aunt isn't very **s**________. She doesn't enjoy being with other people.
6 That actor is so **h**________ and all his children are beautiful, too!
7 More new clothes? You always look so **t**________!
8 My grandma always gives things to other people. She is very **g**________.

3 Read the conversation between two friends and for each question, choose the correct answer, A, B or C.

Jane: Hi, Emily. Have you seen that new (1) ___ at school?

Emily: Yes, what about him?

Jane: Well, his clothes are amazing! The other kids at school aren't so (2) ___. I think he's very beautiful, you know, (3) ___. I've heard he draws very well too. He's very (4) ___.

Emily: Well, you've got hundreds of friends! You're normally so (5) ___! Just go and talk to him!

Jane: What do you want me to say?

Emily: Just say 'Hi, my name is Jane. Nice to meet you.' You just have to be (6) ___ when you meet new people, right?

Jane: Sure, but I'm too (7) ___ to talk to him!

Emily: Well, I've got a nice surprise for you! I bought three tickets to the rock concert on Saturday and one of them is a present for you!

Jane: Wow, thanks, that's very (8) ___ of you. But why three tickets? Who's coming with us?

Emily: The new guy!

Jane: WHAT!!! Do you know him?

Emily: Yes, he's my cousin!

	A	B	C
1	sociable	guy	handsome
2	trendy	shy	generous
3	generous	trendy	handsome
4	artistic	shy	funny
5	handsome	artistic	sociable
6	trendy	polite	guy
7	generous	sociable	shy
8	artistic	generous	trendy

4 Match to make sentences.

1 My teacher is so kind and ___
2 Please be sociable and ___
3 Don't you think my brother ___
4 You must be polite ___
5 Me? Draw? No, ___
6 Who's that tall ___
7 Nice clothes! You always ___
8 Don't be ___

a guy over there?
b shy! Call her!
c I'm not artistic at all!
d generous to everyone.
e talk to our guests.
f to the teacher.
g is very handsome?
h look very trendy!

Grammar 1

G

Articles 2

Look again at *Grammar database 19* on page 151 before doing these exercises.

1 **Read the dialogue and write *a*, *an* or *the*. If no article is necessary, put a dash (–).**

Anna: Hey, did you hear (1) ________ news? I got (2) ________ job for the summer.

Tony: That's great. Where are you working? In (3) ________ office?

Anna: No. In (4) ________ shop, a trendy clothes shop!

Tony: Really? Are (5) ________ clothes very expensive?

Anna: Yes, they are, and the people who buy them have got a lot of (6) ________ money! Yesterday (7) ________ guy came in. He was (8) ________ tall, handsome man with long black hair. He spoke (9) ________ Spanish to the lady who was with him. I thought I knew him but I couldn't remember how. Anyway, last night I went to (10) ________ cinema and I saw him again!

Tony: Was he sitting near you? Did you say hello?

Anna: No, I didn't!

Tony: You're always so shy!

Anna: No, that wasn't why! He wasn't watching (11) ________ film. He was in it! He's (12) ________ really famous actor!

Tony: Amazing!

2 **Read the questions and choose the correct answer, a or b.**

1 What does your dad do?
  a He's engineer.
  b He's an engineer.

2 Where does he work?
  a He works in an office.
  b He works in office.

3 Does your mum work too?
  a Yes, she's language teacher.
  b Yes, she's a language teacher.

4 What language does she teach?
  a She teaches Russian and German.
  b She teaches the Russian and the German.

5 Have you got any sisters or brothers?
  a Yes, I've got a brother.
  b Yes, I've got the brother.

6 What does he look like?
  a He's tall and thin with a short dark hair.
  b He's tall and thin with short dark hair.

7 What's he like?
  a Very funny! He's a great guy to hang out with.
  b Very funny! He's great guy to hang out with.

8 Does he work too?
  a Yes, he's in army.
  b Yes, he's in the army.

Wordpower!

1 **Complete the sentences with the correct form of the word in bold.**

1 My brother never remembers my birthday! He's so _________ . **forget**
2 You never get tired! You're very _________ . **energy**
3 My grandfather never thinks anything nice can happen. He's very _________ . **pessimism**
4 Please be very _________ when you use my computer. **care**
5 Mum says that we should be more _________ at home. She says she does all the work! **help**
6 You are very good at sports! Is all your family that _________? **athlete**
7 Wow! What a _________ concert! **wonder**
8 It was very _________ of you to bring me flowers. **thought**

2 **Match each question with its answer.**

1 Who is thoughtful? ___
2 Who is optimistic? ___
3 Who is forgetful? ___
4 Who is athletic? ___
5 Who is artistic? ___
6 Who is energetic? ___

a Jane never remembers anything!
b Boris can play many sports very well.
c Brad always sees the good things about life.
d Sally can draw and paint well.
e Frank thinks about other people and their needs.
f Maria does many things and she never feels tired.

Listening

10

1 **KET** **Listen to the conversation between Julie and Fred. For each question, choose the correct answer, A, B or C.**

A ☐ B ☐ C ☐

1 Which person is Angela?

A ☐ B ☐ C ☐

2 Which person is Angela's father?

A ☐ B ☐ C ☐

3 Where does Angela work?

A ☐ B ☐ C ☐

4 What is Angela's favourite hobby?

Grammar 2 G

Adjectives and adverbs

Look again at *Grammar database 20* on page 152 before doing these exercises.

1 **Choose the correct word or phrase.**

1 Why does Jimmy always speak **loud / loudly** on the phone?
2 My brother is such a **little funny / funny little** guy!
3 Please don't arrive **late / lately** to school again.
4 My sister's got **blonde short / short blonde** hair.
5 Please read the exam question very **careful / carefully**.
6 You work really **hard / hardly**. You never stop!
7 Look at that man's **long red / red long** beard.
8 My dad can speak Chinese very **good / well**.

2 **Complete the sentences using the correct form of the word in bold.**

1 Why did the teacher __________ leave the class? **sudden**
2 It was a __________ idea to invite Jack to your party. **love**
3 I __________ agree that your cousin is very handsome! **total**
4 Yes, I will __________ go to the school dance with you! **happy**
5 You are __________ right. The French are amazing cooks! **complete**
6 My sister sings __________ . **beautiful**
7 When I got a dog, I __________ understood how wonderful pets are. **final**
8 This is a __________ magazine. I buy it every Friday. **week**

3 **Rewrite the sentences using adverbs so that the meaning stays the same.**

1 Dan is a slow driver. *Dan drives slowly.*
2 Sue is a beautiful singer. __________
3 Tim is a bad dancer. __________
4 Olga is a good cook. __________
5 Paul is a quick learner. __________
6 Mike is hard worker. __________

✓ Quick check

4 **Put a line through the incorrect sentence.**

1 Can you speak the Spanish? / Can you speak Spanish?
2 My mum's doctor. / My mum's a doctor.
3 Do you like my new red hat? / Do you like my red new hat?
4 My brother's got black short hair. / My brother's got short black hair.
5 You can draw very good. / You can draw very well.
6 My dad drives carefully. / My dad drives careful.

Writing

1 Read the sentences and underline the adjectives.

1 She's a cheerful person.
2 He isn't very tall.
3 He's got short black hair.
4 She's a happy, optimistic person.

2 Read the sentences and underline the adverbs.

1 She plays the guitar well.
2 He sings beautifully when he's happy.
3 He drives very fast.
4 He talks to me nicely.

3 Read this description of a special person and for each question, choose the correct answer, A, B or C.

My wonderful grandfather

(1) My grandfather is a wonderful person. His name is John but I call him Poppa. He lives with our family and I'm very happy that I can see my grandfather every day. He's 60 years old and I'm only 15 years old, but sometimes he's like my best friend. He's a kind person and he's very helpful if I have a problem and need some advice.

(2) My grandfather is tall and thin, and he's got short brown hair. He hasn't got a beard or a moustache. He says that when he was young he had a big moustache, but my grandmother didn't like it! He's got a happy face and he's always very polite to my friends when they come to my house.

(3) My grandfather is a very athletic person. Often people who are my grandfather's age don't do sports. They aren't very energetic, but my grandfather is different! When he was young, he played football. He still plays football, but now he plays slowly. I usually win when we play together! He is also an artistic person. He loves painting trees and mountains and the sea. He often takes me with him when he paints, and I sit next to him quietly and watch. He talks to me about colours and he very carefully shows me how to paint pictures. We often have ice cream on the way back home! That's the best moment of the day with my grandfather!

1 Paragraph 1 tells the reader ...

A about all the family.
B about the writer's house.
C about the writer's favourite person.

2 Paragraph 2 describes ...

A what the grandfather looks like.
B the grandfather's clothes.
C the grandfather's favourite food.

3 Paragraph 3 describes ...

A things that the grandfather likes doing.
B the grandfather's friends.
C the grandfather's favourite sport.

Check your progress! | Units 9–10

1 **Read the text and for each question, choose the correct answer, A, B or C.**

My friends Zoe and Amy are interesting people. Zoe is quite (1) ________ , as she likes painting and drawing as well as music. Amy is very (2) ________ , as she enjoys playing sport and she likes to keep fit. They're both very (3) ________ people, as they're friendly and good at meeting people. They're both very (4) ________ too, as they're always paying (5) ________ other people's meals. We have great fun together! For Amy's birthday, Zoe and I got her a cake that looked (6) ________ a basketball, as she loves that sport. Zoe and I ate most of it, as Amy's very healthy. She eats a lot of (7) ________ fruit and vegetables and she never drinks (8) ________ drinks, only drinks that are (9) sugar- ________ . But for birthdays, you must have a cake! We even had ice cream too, because it goes very well (10) ________ cake!

	A	B	C
1	**A** handsome	**B** artistic	**C** trendy
2	**A** polite	**B** athletic	**C** beautiful
3	**A** shy	**B** forgetful	**C** sociable
4	**A** generous	**B** optimistic	**C** careful
5	**A** with	**B** for	**C** from
6	**A** from	**B** for	**C** like
7	**A** fresh	**B** frozen	**C** fizzy
8	**A** tasty	**B** fizzy	**C** fresh
9	**A** free	**B** low	**C** less
10	**A** from	**B** with	**C** for

10 marks

2 **Write a word from the box in each gap to complete the dialogue.**

and • but • few • little • lot • lots • many • of

Leslie: Don, what have we got in the fridge that we can use for breakfast?
Don: Let's see. We've got a (11) ________ eggs, some tomatoes and some orange juice. There's a (12) ________ butter left for toast. There's also (13) ________ of ketchup.
Leslie: Hmm, ketchup with breakfast. Not for me.
Don: It's good with potatoes. You've got a (14) ________ of potatoes in the cupboard, (15) ________ you haven't got any oil to fry them in.
Leslie: Yeah, I don't cook a lot (16) ________ food in oil. I like food that's fresh, but I haven't got (17) ________ fresh vegetables in the house right now, just the tomatoes.
Don: We can go to the market near your house. The food they've got is cheap (18) ________ they've got fresh food.
Leslie: Yes, but they're closed on Sundays. We'll just use what we've got then!

8 marks

3 **Choose the correct word or phrase. A dash (–) means no article is necessary.**

19 George's mum is **a** / – teacher at a language school.
20 Martin's got a beard and – / **the** short hair.
21 She wore a **long blue lovely** / **lovely long blue** dress.
22 She chose her words **suddenly** / **carefully** when she spoke to the officer.
23 Rachel can speak **the** / – French very well.
24 That man is wearing a **silly little red** / **red silly little** hat.
25 Denise's father works in **the** / – army.

7 marks

Total: ___ / 25 marks

11

Looking Good!

Reading

1 Read the text quickly and decide if the statements are true (T) or false (F).

1 Angela is reading a book about fashion over the years. T/F
2 Mathew and Angela are talking about girls' fashion only. T/F
3 The fashions they talk about are from the 1960s, 1970s and 1980s. T/F

Matthew: What are you reading, Angela?
Angela: It's a magazine about fashion from the last 50 years. Some of these styles are a bit strange. The way girls wore their hair in the 1960s – it was actually kind of cool!
Matthew: Let me see. Wow, that's a lot of hair on her head!
Angela: I know, it's great! This style was called the 'Beehive'. Girls would put all of their long, thick hair on top of their heads.
Matthew: It looks like a small mountain! I don't think that would be the best style for the summer. I like what the guys are wearing in this photo. They're just wearing plain t-shirts and blue jeans. That looks comfortable and good for the summer. For the girls, though, it doesn't look like it was easy.
Angela: Well, it's not always easy to look good! I think it was different in the 1970s. Look at this photo here. The girls are wearing flowery tops with flared trousers and brown shoes. Their hair looks casual, but it still looks nice. I think that's probably an easy style to create. Really, I think girls' clothes during this time were quite fashionable. What do you think?
Matthew: Yes, I think the girls look OK. But I don't think long hair looks good on the guys in the 1970s. I would hate to have long hair! Their trousers look awful on them too, with those flared bottoms. That's not for me! So, I think the girls' fashion in the 1970s was quite interesting, but I can't say the same for the boys' fashion. I really like the boys' fashion in the 1980s. That's my favourite. The guys had short hair and their clothes were really cool. I really like skinny jeans too. They were quite popular then, and still are today.
Angela: Well, I think the 1980s was a very bad time in fashion for girls! Look at all that curly hair! And it's dyed too. I don't like all that big jewellery, and those jackets – how terrible! Their shoulders don't look normal at all with those shoulder pads inside the jackets.
Matthew: Yeah, I agree with you. I think girls' hair during the 1980s didn't look good and it probably took hours to create. I think a good style is one that's easy to create and also looks really good. Wouldn't you agree?
Angela: Yes, and nobody's got hours in the morning to get ready anyway!

2 Read the dialogue again and write one word in each gap.

1 Matthew thinks boys' clothes in the 1960s were ________ to wear.
2 Angela thinks girls' hair in the 1970s was ________ and nice.
3 Matthew thinks girls' fashion in the 1970s was quite ________ .
4 Matthew likes the 1980s because the guys had ________ hair.
5 Angela thinks that shoulder pads in jackets look ________ .

Wordpower!

3 Which words can describe clothes and which can describe hair? Put the words in the correct column. Some words may go in both columns.

	Hair	Clothes
casual		
colourful		
curly		
dyed		
plain		
skinny		
spiky		
tight		

4 KET For each question, choose the correct answer, A, B or C.

1 I like ___ clothes because they feel comfortable.
A spiky **B** curly **C** casual

2 I also like ___ clothes, particularly bright red tops.
A plain **B** colourful **C** tight

3 I rarely wear ___ clothes, such as clothes that are all white.
A colourful **B** dyed **C** plain

4 I don't like ___ clothes because it's hard to move in them.
A tight **B** plain **C** spiky

5 I also don't like ___ jeans because they're tight at the bottom.
A curly **B** casual **C** skinny

6 I like straight hair, so my hair is never ___ .
A tight **B** colourful **C** curly

7 I haven't got ___ hair because I like my hair colour the way it is.
A spiky **B** colourful **C** dyed

8 When my hair was short, I would put gel in it to make it ___ .
A skinny **B** spiky **C** plain

5 Choose the correct adjective.

My older brother has great style. He sometimes wears (1) **casual / curly** clothes like t-shirts and jeans, but he usually wears a (2) **colourful / plain** white shirt with long sleeves. Sometimes he wears trendy, (3) **spiky / colourful** jackets. He likes to wear trousers that are (4) **tight / plain** around the waist but not at the bottom, as he doesn't like (5) **dyed / skinny** trousers. His hair is short and (6) **plain / spiky**, as he wears gel to make it stand up. It's always straight, as he doesn't like (7) **tight / curly** hair at all. He hasn't got (8) **plain / dyed** hair, as his hair is black and he likes that colour. When I'm older, I hope I will look as good as he does!

Grammar 1

G

Comparatives

Look again at *Grammar database 21* on page 152 before doing these exercises.

1 Put the adjectives into the comparative form.

1 My new coat is ________ (**long**) than my old one.
2 Julie's hat is ________ (**wide**) than Monica's.
3 Fran's hair is much ________ (**curly**) than mine.
4 Her clothes are ________ (**colourful**) than her sister's.
5 Michael's clothing style is ________ (**good**) than Frank's.
6 Sorry, but your new hairstyle is ________ (**bad**) than your old one!

2 Choose the correct word or phrase.

1 George is a lot **tall / taller** than Henry.
2 This pair of jeans is **skinnier / more skinny** than my other pair.
3 We're twins, but my brother is 20 minutes older **than / from** me.
4 Michelle is very **fashionable / more fashionable** and I like her style.
5 Clothing was **more casual / casual** in the 1960s than in the 1920s.
6 Renee is **fast / faster** at getting dressed in the morning than her brother.

3 Write sentences using the comparative.

1 Dan's style / casual / Paul's — *Dan's style is more casual that Paul's.*
2 My mum's hair / straight / mine ________
3 Martin's trousers / not tight / Kevin's ________
4 His suit / formal / Fred's t-shirt and jeans ________
5 Her earrings / big / Jill's ________
6 This dress / long / my other one ________
7 Cindy / bad / her sister at getting dressed ________
8 Mike / good / Ralph at shopping ________

4 Write a word from the box in each gap in the comparative form. Add any other words you need (such as *than*).

cool • happy • important • long • old • tall

It's funny. I'm one year (1) ________ my sister, but she's very tall for her age. In fact, she's even (2) ________ me! This of course means I can't wear her clothes. It's too bad because I really like some of her jeans. Her style is much (3) ________ mine, I would say! But her jeans are a lot (4) ________ my legs and it looks funny when I try them on. So, I don't wear them. I think it's (5) ________ to wear clothes that fit than to wear clothes that are cool. So, I think I'm (6) ________ wearing my own clothes!

Wordpower!

1 Each of the words in bold is in the wrong sentence. Write a word in bold from another sentence to replace the incorrect one.

1 You should **have** off that hat because it doesn't look nice. __________
2 You can **leave** up your coat in the wardrobe if you like. __________
3 When my sister and I were young, we would **take** up in our mother's clothes. __________
4 My friends are the guys over there who **do** got suits on. __________
5 He asked to take her coat, but she decided to **try** it on. __________
6 Your shoelaces are not tied and you need to **put** them up. __________
7 These trousers are really big, so I think I'll **hang** a belt on. __________
8 I'm going to **dress** on these boots and if I like them, I'll buy them! __________

2 Write *off*, *on* or *up* in each gap to complete the dialogue.

Jenny: Did you dress (1) __________ for Sheila's party the other night?
Tina: No, I didn't. I tried (2) __________ a few things at the shops, but I didn't like anything. In the end, I just put (3) __________ a skirt, a white t-shirt and a jacket.
Jenny: Oh, well, that's OK. What did other people at the party have (4) __________ ?
Tina: Mike came as a weird scientist. At one point he fell over because he forgot to do his shoelaces (5) __________ .
Jenny: That sounds like something a weird scientist would do, right? Was he OK?
Tina: Oh, sure. Lucy came as a big yellow bird. But it was a bit hot at the party, so she took the costume (6) __________ .
Jenny: Wait, what was she wearing then? Nothing?
Tina: Ha, ha! No, she was wearing clothes under the costume, of course. I told her she should leave the costume (7) __________ because it was a good costume, but I was a bit hot too, and I hung my jacket (8) __________ in Sheila's wardrobe.
Jenny: Maybe it's better to have fancy dress parties in the winter!
Tina: I agree!

Listening

11

1 Listen to a young woman talking to a shop assistant. Write one word in each gap.

1 Karen is thinking of buying a __________ dress.
2 The shop assistant shows Karen dresses that are very __________ .
3 The dresses come in three different colours: blue, green and __________ .
4 After trying on the first dress, Karen needs a dress in a __________ size.
5 The shop assistant offers Karen the same dress in the colour __________ .
6 Karen thought the first dress was only a little too __________ .

Grammar 2 G

Comparatives and superlatives

Look again at *Grammar database 22* on page 152 before doing these exercises.

1 Put the adjectives into the superlative form.

John: Who's (1) __________ (**stylish**) person in your family?

Dina: That would be my sister Lisa. She wears (2) __________ (**good**) clothes and (3) __________ (**fashionable**) accessories. What about in your family?

John: That's easy – me! I'm not particularly stylish, but my brother's got (4) __________ (**bad**) style in clothes. We went shopping yesterday, and he wanted to buy a belt. It was (5) __________ (**ugly**) belt I've ever seen!

Dina: How funny! Did he buy it?

John: Well, he saw another belt, which was (6) __________ (**cheap**) one in the shop. That's the one he got, but I can't say it was nice!

2 Write sentences using the superlative.

1 That / small hat / in the world *That's the smallest hat in the world.*
2 That / lovely dress / I've ever seen __________
3 This / large clothing shop / in town __________
4 These / comfortable shoes / that we sell __________
5 This / not good costume / for the party __________

3 ➲ KET Read the text and for each question, choose the correct word or phrase, A, B or C.

Some people care too much about clothes. To them, clothes are the (1) ___ things in their lives. They often buy (2) ___ shoes in the shop or the (3) ___ fashions of the year. They usually like items that are (4) ___ than casual clothes and (5) ___ just plain white. They are only (6) ___ when they've got money to spend.
Of course, you don't have to spend lots of money to have nice items. It's (7) ___ to shop carefully than to just buy (8) ___ thing you can find. If you buy clothes that are (9) ___ than expensive clothes but look the same, you'll be able to buy more clothes. It's also (10) ___ to buy things you need than things you want. In other words, if you've already got two coats, it's probably not the (11) ___ idea to buy one more!

	A	B	C
1	**A** important	**B** more important	**C** most important
2	**A** most expensive	**B** more expensive	**C** the most expensive
3	**A** newer	**B** newest	**C** more new
4	**A** smart	**B** smarter	**C** smartest
5	**A** more colourful	**B** colourful	**C** more colourful than
6	**A** happy	**B** happier	**C** happiest
7	**A** good	**B** better	**C** best
8	**A** the coolest	**B** the cooler	**C** cool
9	**A** cheaper than	**B** cheap	**C** cheaper
10	**A** useful	**B** more useful	**C** most useful
11	**A** great	**B** greater	**C** greatest

Quick check

4 **Choose the correct answer.**

1 Do we use the comparative to talk about things that are different from other things? **yes / no**
2 Which is correct? **She's shorter than Martin. / She's more short than Martin. / both**
3 Do we use the superlative to compare two things or more than two things?
two things / more than two things
4 Do we use the superlative to say something is at the top or bottom of a group?
top / bottom / both
5 Which is correct? **He's the best student in class. / He's the best in class. / both**

Writing

1 **Read the poster quickly and choose the correct answers.**

1 **Shop assistants / Models** will be wearing the clothes at the fashion show.
2 Some clothes at the fashion show are for **casual wear / the office**.
3 The fashion show takes places at a **department store / shopping centre**.

Easton Shopping Centre
proudly presents

FASHION WEEKEND!

Join us at Easton Shopping Centre's fashion event of the year!

Watch our professional fashion models present:

- the latest trends in formal wear
- the most stylish suits for today's business world
- the loveliest evening dresses
- the most colourful jewellery and accessories
- the most fantastic shoes for a nice evening

and so much more!

West Entrance, Easton Shopping Centre
Saturday and Sunday,
30th & 31st May, 1–4pm

★★★★★★★★★★★★★★★★★★★★★★

Entrance: £12
Refreshments included

★★★★★★★★★★★★★★★★★★★★★★

Many thanks to Lewis Department Store for kindly providing all the clothes, shoes and accessories.

2 **Read the poster again and for each question, choose the correct answer A, B or C.**

1 The fashion show at Easton Shopping Centre happens every ...
A day.
B week.
C year.

2 The fashion show will probably display ...
A plain t-shirts.
B shirts.
C blue jeans.

3 The show will also display dresses for ...
A casual wear.
B the beach.
C a formal event.

4 The shoes at the show will probably be ...
A sporty.
B cheap.
C formal.

5 Which of the following is free at the event?
A food and drink
B items of clothing
C neither

12

It's a Goal!

Reading

1 ➲ KET Read the five texts and match them to the statements (a–e).

a Choose a sport that matches your character.
b My team is doing very well!
c Do things slowly and carefully.
d Meet new people while you get fit.
e This student will not be in class.

1 ___

Do you want to **GET FIT**?

Now's the perfect time to take up a new sport, meet new friends and feel better!

– If you are under 18 years old, you will get our special student price for one year!
– Come and visit the gym today and make new friends!
– We have gymnastics, judo classes and a beautiful new indoor pool!

We are open every day of the week - just for you!

2 ___

Dear Peter,
I think your idea of taking up a sport is a very good idea! You said in your email to us that you spend many hours in front of the computer and that you don't think you're in good shape. Well, it's good to hear that you want to get fit, but you must be careful. When many people join a gym, they do too much exercise in the first week and this is not good. If you do things slowly, it'll be much better for you. Be patient. Please keep in touch and tell us how it goes.
Good luck!
Dr Scott

3 ___

Dear Mr Thomas,
This is a note to say that my daughter Jenny will not be able to come to school on Friday. Jenny is a member of a gymnastics team and on Friday her team will take part in a gymnastics competition. If you give homework for the weekend, her classmates will tell her what to do.
Thank you,
Mrs Jackson

4 ___

write reply send

Hey, Tony!

Guess what? We won! It was amazing – the score was 2–2 and all the spectators were shouting and screaming 'Go Danny! Go Danny!' and I kicked the ball really hard and scored! So, we beat the other team 2–3. HAHAHA. This is really good news because now our team will play in the final next weekend! Can you come and watch that match? Come on! We need everyone on our side!

Talk later,

Danny

5 ___

If you want to take up a new sport, here are two things to think about.

Do you like being indoors or outdoors? Some sports, such as skiing or football, are usually played outdoors, but other sports can be played indoors.

Another important question is: do I like being part of a team or do I like doing sports alone? Tennis is a sport where you are on your own. Basketball is a team sport, of course, so you need to work closely with other players on your team.

What kind of sport is better for **YOUR** character? You decide!

Wordpower!

2 **Write a word or phrase in each gap to complete the sentences. The first letter is given to help you.**

1 If you want to swim more quickly, you will have to **t**_________ very hard every day.
2 Many of the **s**_________ were very upset when their team lost the game.
3 The team who wins the football **f**_________ will be the best team in the world!
4 I need to **g**_________ **f**_________! I sit at a computer for too many hours at work.
5 The noise in the football **s**_________ was amazing when the player scored the final goal!
6 I think I'll **t**_________ **u**_________ skiing this winter. I've always loved the snow.
7 I've got two tickets for the basketball **m**_________ this weekend. Do you want to come?
8 Last year, I couldn't **t**_________ **p**_________ in any sport because I had no free time.

3 **Read the story and for each question, choose the correct answer, A, B or C.**

I'll never forget something that happened to me when I was 16 years old. I thought that it was time to (1) ____. All my friends were (2) ____ in sports or going to the gym every day so I thought it was a good idea to do the same. Well, I decided to (3) ____ football. I was a fast runner and it was fun hanging out with all the other players. Anyway, our team (4) ____ very hard every day and we won enough games to play in the (5) ____! On the day of the big (6) ____ we were very nervous. There were hundreds of people in the (7) ____. With two minutes left, the score was 2-2. The ball came to me and I kicked it as hard as I could. The ball went the wrong way and the (8) ____ went silent. I looked around and saw why – I had scored a goal for the other team!

	A	B	C
1	**A** get fit	**B** get up	**C** do fit
2	**A** doing	**B** taking part	**C** taking up
3	**A** put up	**B** get up	**C** take up
4	**A** trained	**B** took up	**C** took part
5	**A** final	**B** game	**C** sport
6	**A** spectator	**B** stadium	**C** match
7	**A** stadium	**B** match	**C** final
8	**A** match	**B** stadium	**C** spectators

Grammar 1 G

Zero and first conditional

Look again at *Grammar database 23* on page 153 before doing these exercises.

1 **Read the sentences. Write ZC for zero conditional or FC for first conditional.**

1 If the weather is sunny, we'll play basketball outdoors. ___
2 If you join the swimming team, you'll have to train after school. ___
3 If I do exercise every day, I feel more energetic. ___
4 If the team trains every day, they'll win the competition. ___
5 If the ball touches the ground, you lose a point. ___
6 If you want to get fit, you'll have to join a gym. ___
7 If you take part in a team sport, you'll make new friends. ___
8 If you take up running, you need special shoes. ___

2 **For each question, choose the correct answer, a or b.**

1 If you do exercise every day, ...
a you'll feel better.
b you're feeling better.

2 If you hit the ball outside, ...
a the other player wins a point.
b the other player to win a point.

3 If you decide to join the gym, ...
a I join too.
b I'll join too.

4 If the players train hard for the final, ...
a I'm sure they'll win.
b I'm sure they win.

5 If it rains next Saturday, ...
a they play indoors.
b they'll play indoors.

3 **Read the email from Shelly to her friend and choose the correct phrase.**

write reply send

To: Lucy Thornton <lucy4ever@fastmail.com>
Subject: Sports

Hey, Lucy,

I need your advice. I really want to join a sports team this year, but I don't know which one to choose. I like team sports, but if (1) **I join / I'll join** the basketball team, I will have to practise three times a week. And I'm worried, because if (2) **I'll spend / I spend** so many hours doing sports, (3) **I'll be / I am** too tired to do my homework. I want to do well in the exams this year, but if (4) **I am / I'll be** always tired, (5) **I do / I'll do** badly at school. I talked to my teacher. She said I should take up a sport that isn't a team sport. She said if (6) **I'll take up / I take up** tennis, I can practise when I'm free. I think that's a good idea. What do you think?

Talk later,

Shelly

Wordpower!

1 Write a word from the box in each gap.

beat • do • go • learn • play • score • train • win

1 Would you like to __________ horse-riding this weekend?
2 We lost 2-0! Our team didn't __________ any goals at all!
3 I'm sure our basketball team will __________ your team this year!
4 Do you know how to __________ tennis?
5 I would love to __________ judo, but I'm afraid I'll get hurt!
6 I have to __________ hard for the gymnastics competition next week.
7 Who do you think will __________ the match this year? Our school or yours?
8 Amazing! When did you __________ how to ski? You're really good!

2 Read the conversation between two friends and choose the correct word.

Paul: Hey, Ruby! Have you ever (1) **trained / been** horse-riding?
Ruby: No, I haven't. Why?
Paul: There's a riding school not far from the city. I'd love to (2) **learn / play** how to ride.
Ruby: Really? I can't imagine you on a horse! Anyway, you haven't got any time next week. You have to (3) **train / score** for the match.
Paul: Yes, I guess you're right. And the other team is going to (4) **beat / win** us if we don't improve. Did you see that tall player they have? He's amazing!
Ruby: You mean the guy who (5) **scored / did** five goals in the last game? I think everyone noticed him! He (6) **trains / does** judo too, you know.
Paul: What? Are you serious?
Ruby: And he (7) **plays / scores** baseball too!
Paul: Oh, no! The other team is going to (8) **win / beat** the match – I can feel it already!

Listening

12

1 KET Listen to a man calling a sports centre and complete the information.

- **Name of the Gym:** *Get Fit Gym*
- **Address:** 290 __________ Road
- **Special price is:** __________ a month for one year
- **Buses for the gym:** number 9, 14B and __________
- **Opening hours for the gym:** from __________ until 11pm
- **Telephone number for the pools:** __________

12

2 Listen again and for each question, choose the correct answer, a or b.

1 The small swimming pool is for ...
a children younger than 10.
b children younger than 12.

2 Twice a week, the swimming pools close at ...
a six o'clock.
b seven o'clock.

3 If you want to have tennis lessons ...
a you must pay more.
b you don't have to pay more.

4 The man talking on the phone ...
a wants to find a job.
b has already got a job.

Grammar 2

G

Second conditional

Look again at *Grammar database 24* on page 153 before doing these exercises.

1 Write the verbs in the correct form.

1 If there __was__ a pool at my school, I __would learn__ to swim. (**be / learn**)
2 If I ________ more time, I ______________ the basketball team. (**have / join**)
3 If you ________ every day, you ______________ quickly. (**train / get fit**)
4 If I ________ near the sea, I ______________ windsurfing. (**live / take up**)
5 If I ________ a famous sports player, I'm sure I ______________ shy. (**meet / feel**)
6 If the tickets to the final match ________ cheaper, I ______________. (**be / go**)
7 If our school ________ more money, we ______________ a new stadium. (**have / build**)
8 If you ________ goggles in the pool, your eyes ______________. (**wear / not hurt**)

2 Read the dialogue and choose the correct word or phrase.

Maria: I'm so tired! I don't understand it. I don't usually go to bed very late.
Tim: Well, here's some important advice for you. Maybe you should take up a sport. If you (1) **did / doing** exercise every day, I'm sure you (2) **would / can** feel happier and more energetic.
Maria: If I (3) **would go / went** to the gym, I (4) **will / would** get fit quickly.
Tim: So, what are you waiting for? Let's go today after school.
Maria: But everyone at the gym is already in good shape. If I (5) **am / was** in good shape, I (6) **didn't / wouldn't** feel shy.
Tim: Well, all these people weren't fit a few months ago either, you know.
Maria: If there (7) **is / was** a pool at the gym, I (8) **am / would** train every day! I love swimming.
Tim: Well, guess what? A new pool opened last week and it's amazing.
Maria: OK, that's it! I'm going to join that gym today!

✔ Quick check

3 Put a line through the incorrect sentence.

1 If you want to be a professional footballer, you will have to practise a lot. / If you want to be a professional footballer, you practise a lot.
2 Today is your birthday so if you tell me what you want to do, I do it. / Today is your birthday so if you tell me what you want to do, I'll do it.
3 If I had more money, I would take up windsurfing. / If I have more money, I would take up windsurfing.
4 If you did sports more often, you would to feel healthier. / If you did sports more often, you would feel healthier.
5 If there was a gym near my house, I would work out very often. / If there was gym near my house, I will work out very often.

Writing

1 Read the sentences. Underline the passive form.

1 Special goggles are used to protect the skier's eyes from the sun.
2 Gloves are worn to protect the snowboarder's hands if he falls.
3 A helmet is needed to protect the cyclist if she falls off her bike.
4 The snowboard is used to ride down the mountain.
5 The match is played in the big stadium every year.

2 Read this description of a sport and for each question, choose the correct answer, A, B or C.

1 Paragraph 1 tells the reader ...
A general information about snowboarding.
B events in the Winter Olympics.
C that dangerous people enjoy snowboarding.

2 Paragraph 2 describes ...
A the clothes that snowboarders wear.
B things you need to do this sport.
C the best weather for snowboarding.

3 Paragraph 3 describes ...
A the writer's personal experience of the sport.
B things that snowboarders do in competitions.
C the rules of snowboarding.

An exciting sport

(1) A sport that I love is snowboarding. Snowboarding is a new sport. It only started about forty years ago, but now it's very popular all around the world. Today, snowboarding is even included in the Winter Olympics. People who love surfing in the sea or skateboarding often love snowboarding. It is a fast, exciting sport, but it can also be very dangerous.

(2) To do snowboarding you really only need two things. You need a snowy mountain and a board. But because snowboarders ride their boards over the snow very fast, they can get hurt badly if they fall off. So, snowboarders also need to wear a helmet on their heads. This protects their heads if they hit the ground hard. They must also wear gloves so their hands are protected and special clothes to protect their knees. Finally, they must always wear powerful goggles to protect their eyes from the bright sun.

(3) Snowboarding is not a team sport where there are rules to a game. It is an individual sport and the winner of a competition must be able to do many different things. In some snowboarding events, the athlete has to jump very high in the air and stay on the board. In other events, the snowboarder has to ride very fast between posts and at the same time to go down the side of a very big mountain. The interesting thing about snowboarding is that new events and new rules are created all the time. Snowboarders are people who love adventure. They are always trying to find more exciting and more dangerous things to do.

Check your progress! | Units 11–12

1 Read the sentences and for each question, choose the correct answer, A, B or C.

1 You don't need to wear anything special to the party tonight. Most people will wear ___ clothes.

A curly B casual C tight

2 I don't like wearing ___ clothes. I like plain colours.

A colourful B skinny C dyed

3 Why don't you ___ your jacket? It's very hot in here.

A dress up B tie up C take off

4 I think you should ___ these jeans before you buy them. They might not be your size.

A try on B put on C hang up

5 If you want to be an amazing football player, you have to ___ every day.

A train B take up C take part

6 All the ___ in the stadium were wearing the colours of their team.

A match B final C spectators

7 If my team plays well, I'm sure we'll ___ your team today!

A win B beat C score

8 Where did you ___ how to swim? You're much better than me!

A play B go C learn

8 marks

2 Complete the conversation using the comparative or the superlative form of the adjective.

Mike: Hey, Vicki, you're an amazing runner. You're the (9) ________ (**fast**) athlete in the school! Do other people in your family do sports too?

Vicki: Yes, we all do! Of course my dad's (10) ________ (**old**) than me, but he's (11) ________ (**fast**) than all of us!

Mike: Does your mum run too?

Vicki: No, she swims. She was the (12) ________ (**good**) swimmer in her school when she was young.

Mike: And your brother?

Vicki: He plays basketball. He's the (13) ________ (**tall**) person in the team but other kids are (14) ________ (**good**) players than him. But Mum says he's the (15) ________ (**lazy**) person in our family!

Mike: Does he ever help with cooking?

Vicki: Yes, sometimes. But he's the (16) ________ (**bad**) cook in the world! But don't tell him I said that, please!

8 marks

3 Complete the sentences with the correct conditional form of the verb.

17 If I ________ (**have**) more money, I would buy those lovely earrings.

18 If I ________ (**know**) the rules of ice hockey, I would enjoy it more.

19 Would Peter come shopping with us next weekend if he ________ (**have**) some free time?

20 If you ________ (**buy**) this hat, you can wear it to the party on Saturday.

21 If I ________ (**know**) more about fashion, I would wear trendier clothes.

22 If those new trousers ________ (**be**) too long, you'll fall over when you walk!

23 If my mum had more free time, she ________ (**take up**) a sport.

24 If we ________ (**live**) closer to a swimming pool, I would train every weekend.

25 If you wanted to, you ________ (**can**) be the best player of the team.

9 marks

Total: ___ / 25 marks

13

Right Time, Right Place!

Reading

1 Read the article quickly and choose the correct answer.

1 This article is mainly about **train travel / train stations**.
2 The places mentioned in the article are in **Europe / America**.
3 The places mentioned in the article opened in the **1800s / 1900s**.

Europe's Busiest Train Stations

Trains are a very common form of transport, particularly in Europe. Millions of people travel by train in Europe every year, making Europe's train stations a popular meeting spot for travellers. Two stations in particular are quite busy, but they are busy in different ways.

In Paris, the Gare du Nord, or 'North Station', is Europe's busiest train station by the number of people who get on and off trains. A total of 190 million people leave from or arrive at this station every year. The first station opened on 14th June 1846, but after a few years, the managers of the train lines decided it was too small. The old station was destroyed and a new, larger station opened in 1864. The station was finished in 1865, but people could still use the station while workers finished building it.

The station in Europe that's got the most trains passing through it is Clapham Junction in south London. The station opened on 2nd March 1863, a little earlier than when the larger Gare du Nord opened. Today, about 2,000 trains pass through Clapham Junction every day. During its busiest times, over 170 trains pass through this train station in one hour or about three trains every minute. Because some trains don't stop, there are fewer people that pass through this station than the Gare du Nord.

2 KET Read the article again and for each question, choose the correct answer, A, B or C.

1 The article is about two different train stations in Europe.
A Right
B Wrong
C Doesn't say

2 More people pass through the Gare du Nord than any other station.
A Right
B Wrong
C Doesn't say

3 About 190 million people have passed through the Gare du Nord since it opened.
A Right
B Wrong
C Doesn't say

4 People started to use the new Gare du Nord in 1865.
A Right
B Wrong
C Doesn't say

5 Clapham Junction was a very busy station when it opened.
A Right
B Wrong
C Doesn't say

6 More trains pass through Clapham Junction than the Gare du Nord.
A Right
B Wrong
C Doesn't say

7 Less people leave from and arrive at Clapham Junction than at the Gare du Nord.
A Right
B Wrong
C Doesn't say

Wordpower!

3 Match each word or phrase with its definition.

1	This says where something is when it's facing something else. ___	**a**	above
2	This can mean 'exactly' or 'directly'. ___	**b**	wrong
3	This describes something that is the most important or the biggest. ___	**c**	opposite
4	This can mean to persuade someone to do something. ___	**d**	on time
5	When you don't arrive late for something, you're this. ___	**e**	right
6	This describes something that's not correct. ___	**f**	main
7	This says where something is when it's on top of something else. ___	**g**	get

4 Write a word from the box in each gap.

above • main • opposite • right

Living in the city centre is fun. I live on the (1) __________ street in my town, so there's lots of things to do. My parents own a bookshop, and we live (2) __________ it, on the first floor. We also live (3) __________ a theatre, so if I want to see a play, I can just go across the street! Our flat is also (4) __________ by a cinema, so it's easy to watch films too. With all this entertainment, who would want to live somewhere else?

5 Read the dialogue and choose the correct word.

Sarah: Hi, Gordon. I just (1) **got / took** to the shopping centre. Where are you?

Gordon: I'm at the café (2) **right / opposite** *Darrel's Books.* Do you know where that is?

Sarah: Not really, but there's a map at the (3) **above / main** entrance of the shopping centre. Have you been here long?

Gordon: Oh, about 30 minutes. I (4) **made / got** my mum to drive me here early. I wanted to be sure I made it to the film (5) **past / on** time.

Sarah: You're here very early. The film doesn't start for another hour.

Gordon: Wait, I thought it started at 6.30?

Sarah: No, that's the (6) **right / wrong** time. It starts at 7.

Gordon: That's strange. I'm looking at the paper, and it says (7) **right / opposite** here that *The Escape* starts at 6.30.

Sarah: Oh, I thought we were going to see *The Postcard.*

Gordon: That's not showing at this cinema. If you look at the sign (8) **above / right** the cinema, it says there's only one film, *The Escape.*

Sarah: Oh, I must have made a mistake. Oh, well, I guess that's the film we're seeing!

Grammar 1

G

Prepositions of time and place

Look again at *Grammar database 25* on page 153 before doing these exercises.

1 Tick (✔) the sentence where the word in bold is correct. If it's wrong, write the correct word.

1 Do you want to meet **at** Tuesday? ________
2 Lisa waited for Greg **in** an hour. ________
3 I'll be home **in** five minutes to watch the film. ________
4 The shopping centre opens **on** 9am. ________
5 My favourite band is playing **at** Friday night. ________
6 The meeting doesn't start **in** another half-hour. ________
7 I'll be standing in front **to** the chemist. ________
8 What's the busiest train station **on** the world? ________
9 Meet me at the café next **to** the cinema. ________
10 They rode home **by** their bikes. ________

2 Write a word from the box in each gap to complete the text.

at • above • by • in • in front near • next • outside • to

Jake, I'm arriving (1) ________ Manchester today and I'm coming (2) ________ train. Can you pick me up (3) ________ the station? I'll wait for you (4) ________ to the newsagent's. I think the newsagent's is (5) ________ the main entrance. I'm not quite sure though. Do you prefer to meet at the café (6) ________ the information desk? From up there, I can easily see you coming. If you decide to take the car, there's a car park right (7) ________ of the main entrance. You know what? Call me when you get (8) ________ the station and I'll meet you (9) ________.
Claire

3 Choose the correct word or phrase. A dash (–) means no preposition is necessary.

Frank: Have you been (1) **to / at** Aberdeen, Julie?

Julie: Yes, I went there (2) **in / on** 2004. It was (3) **during / behind** my summer holidays.

Frank: My family and I are going (4) **in / on** a journey there this year. Did you enjoy it?

Julie: I liked the town, but I didn't like the hotel. When we walked (5) **next to / into** our room, we saw that it wasn't clean. My dad walked (6) **out of / over** the room right away to speak to the manager. We got another room, but it was right (7) **outside / above** a busy café. I guess we were staying (8) **for / in** the wrong hotel!

Frank: Hmm. That's too bad. How was the town?

Julie: Good. We stayed (9) **in / to** the town centre, so it was easy to get around. My favourite place was this music shop (10) **behind / in front** the local supermarket. They had these really cool instruments that were over a hundred years old.

Frank: Wow, that is cool! Were the restaurants nice?

Julie: Yes, they were. One place was particularly interesting. It was right (11) **next / outside** the fish market. The food was really fresh and tasty.

Frank: It sounds like you had a good trip. Too bad about the hotel, though.

Julie: Yes, I enjoyed the trip, but I was ready to go (12) **to / –** home!

Wordpower!

1 Match to make sentences.

1 She called to make ___
2 Have you made ___
3 Please do ___
4 Don't hurry – just take ___
5 Will you drive to your parents' house or take ___
6 Will you have ___

a a party at the weekend?
b the dishes before you watch TV.
c your time.
d an appointment for tomorrow.
e a bus?
f plans for your holiday?

2 ➲ KET Read the text and for each question, choose the correct answer, A, B or C.

To: Sharon Myers <lovelysharon@fastmail.com>
Subject: Where to have the party?

Hi, Sharon,

I wanted to ask you about this weekend's party. Are we (1) ___ the party on Saturday? It seems I've (2) ___ a mistake. Saturday is such a busy day for me! John's (3) ___ a train to Oxford and I have to drive him to the station. Also, my house isn't clean and I have to (4) ___ a lot of housework. So, can you (5) ___ me a big favour? Is it OK to use your house for the party? I'll (6) ___ my best to help you. Let me know if you need help (7) ___ plans. I can call to (8) ___ an arrangement for the food if you like.

What do you think?

Bye now,

Liz

	A	B	C
1	taking	having	making
2	had	done	made
3	taking	doing	having
4	make	do	take
5	take	do	make
6	make	have	do
7	doing	taking	making
8	have	make	do

Listening

13

1 ➲ KET Listen to four short dialogues and for each question, choose the correct answer, A, B or C.

A ☐ B ☐ C ☐

1 How will Mark travel?

A ☐ B ☐ C ☐

2 What time will Stephen arrive at Rebecca's house?

A ☐ B ☐ C ☐

3 What day is Samantha visiting George?

A ☐ B ☐ C ☐

4 Where are Frank and Jenny meeting?

Grammar 2

G

Present perfect simple 3

Look again at *Grammar database 26* on page 154 before doing these exercises.

1 **Write *for* or *since* in each gap to complete the dialogue.**

Chris: Paula, where are you? I've been at the restaurant (1) ________ over an hour.

Paula: Sorry, I'm still at the supermarket. I've been in line (2) ________ 20 minutes. They're very busy.

Chris: Oh, Paula! Did you have to go to the supermarket before lunch? I've been here (3) ________ 12 o'clock. I don't think the waiter's happy. He's been right by my table (4) ________ the past 10 minutes. I think I should leave.

Paula: Maybe that's a good idea. I'm really sorry for the wait. Why don't you meet me at that new place near the supermarket? It's only been open (5) ________ July. It seems nice.

Chris: OK, but you're buying lunch!

Paula: Yes, I should do that. OK, let's get off the phone. We've been talking (6) ________ more than five minutes!

Chris: OK. See you soon, I hope!

2 **Write a word from the box in each gap to complete the text.**

2008 • been • for • has • two • week

I've lived in New York since (1) ________ and I'm really enjoying it. I'm particularly excited this week because my friend Barbara is visiting. She's been here (2) ________ four days now and she really likes it. We've (3) ________ to many places around town. We went to the Statue of Liberty, where we waited for (4) ________ hours to get in. It was terrific, though. I also took Barbara to this great art show that (5) ________ been here since the spring. Barbara's here for one more (6) ________ , then she goes back to England. I'll miss her, but I'm glad I'm staying here!

3 **Write sentences using *for* or *since*.**

1 Sally / live in Scotland / five months
Sally's lived in Scotland for five months.

2 Jason / have a pet bird / October
____

3 Leslie / be in the kitchen / a quarter past two
____

4 Neil / live in Brighton / 1997
____

5 Vicky / have the tickets / weeks now
____

6 Blake / be in class / an hour and a half
____

Quick check

4 Choose the correct answer.

1 Do we use prepositions before times, places, or both? **times / places / both**
2 Which is correct? **We'll go on foot. / We'll go by foot. / both**
3 Which is correct? **I'm at home. / I'm at the home. / both**
4 Do we use *for* with the present perfect simple to show when a situation – which is still continuing – started? **yes / no**
5 Do we use *since* with the present perfect simple to show how long a situation has continued? **yes / no**
6 Which is correct? **I've been here since 5pm. / I've been here since two hours. / both**

Writing

1 Read the email and decide if the statements are true (T) or false (F).

write reply send

To: Michelle Reynolds <michellereynolds@quickmail.com>
Subject: Christmas holidays

Hi, Michelle!

(1) Thanks for your email. I'm glad it's almost winter break too. It'll be nice to be out of school!

(2) So, it sounds like you're going to have some free time after Christmas to come for a visit. That's great! I'll be happy to see you! I really miss all my friends. (I've lived here since June and no-one's visited me yet, so I'm glad you're coming!)

(3) Here's what I suggest. Why don't you come on Wednesday 27th December in the afternoon? You can take the train from Liverpool to Edinburgh. It takes about four hours, so be sure to get a morning train. I'll meet you at the station.

(4) On Wednesday evening, we'll go out for pizza in my neighbourhood (there's an excellent pizza place near my house). Then we can decide what to do for the rest of the week. We can go to the cinema, or we can visit the castle. It's really cool, you'll love it! What do you think?

Bye for now!

Ellen

1 Ellen's lived in Edinburgh for two years. T/F
2 Ellen hasn't seen any of her friends since she moved to Edinburgh. T/F
3 Ellen wants Michelle to arrive in the afternoon. T/F
4 The girls will make all the plans before Michelle arrives. T/F

2 Read the email again and match each main paragraph with a statement. There is one statement you do not need to use.

1 Paragraph 1 ___
2 Paragraph 2 ___
3 Paragraph 3 ___
4 Paragraph 4 ___

a This paragraph describes Michelle's travel arrangements.
b This paragraph describes what Ellen has done in school this year.
c This paragraph talks about how Ellen feels about Michelle's visit.
d This paragraph makes a comment about not having to go to school.
e This paragraph talks about the girls' plans while Michelle is visiting.

14

Words and Pictures!

Reading

1 ➲ **KET These five texts are comments from the same blog. Read the five comments and match them to the names (a–e).**

a I need a job
b Cameraman
c Save-the-forests reader
d Techno-Grandpa
e News for everyone

People who say that old people are afraid of technology are wrong! I am 72 years old and I love computers. Every morning while I have breakfast, I go online and read five different newspapers – all on the internet. It's my favourite time of the day! Sitting in my kitchen with my cup of coffee, I can read about news events in every country around the world. Remember, older people often have health problems. People who are my age can't walk to the shop easily to buy newspapers. News online is perfect for us!

1 Comment by ___

Why do we still print newspapers? I have no idea! Think about it – what is paper made from? Trees, of course! Every day, newspapers print thousands of copies of newspapers for their readers, but all this paper comes from trees. This is why we need to use the internet for our news. There are so many wonderful newspapers online – and these online sites do not DESTROY trees! NO MORE NEWSPAPERS from PAPER is what I say!

2 Comment by ___

I love reading the newspaper, watching TV and visiting online news sites, but what about all the readers who do not have the money to buy a beautiful new iPad™ or computer? What about all the people on this planet who do not even have electricity in their homes? There are so many places in the world where you cannot get the internet! People all over the planet should be able to read the news. I agree that we destroy trees to print newspapers, but the media must try to inform **EVERYONE** – not only the lucky people who have the money to buy nice computers.

3 Comment by ___

For the last five years, I have worked as a sports journalist with a local newspaper and today I lost my job. The editor of the newspaper said that sales have dropped and we do not sell enough copies of our paper to survive. Online news sites are more popular nowadays and a lot of people who work in the media are losing their jobs. I am so worried. I wonder where I can find another job soon!?

4 Comment by ___

Change is great! Online newspapers are much better than newspapers! Why? Because when we use online newspapers we can **READ** the news and **WATCH** the news! This is fantastic. I'm not young, but I have learned how to use a computer and in my opinion online news is amazing. I used to be a photographer and of course I love watching videos of news. **SEEING** something is much more powerful than just reading about it. Humans love watching other humans and with video clips on news websites we can do this every minute of the day. Newspapers are for the past! Internet news is for the present.

5 Comment by ___

Wordpower!

2 Write a word in each gap to complete the sentences. The first letter is given to help you.

1 How many **c**________ of this newspaper are sold every week?
2 Do you want me to **p**________ all these pages?
3 Many **r**________ use online newspapers because they're faster and cheaper.
4 I'd like to **i**________ you that you've got the job!
5 You have to be very energetic to work in **t**________ **m**________ – news changes every minute!
6 I love writing! I think I'd like to be a **j**________ one day.
7 The **e**________ of the newspaper decides which news stories to include every day.
8 If you **c**________ here you will see great video clips about today's news.

3 Read this article from a newspaper and for each question, choose the correct answer, A, B or C.

Thank you and Goodbye!

This is a short message from the (1) ___ of this newspaper to all our wonderful (2) ___ who have bought our newspaper for years. We are very sorry to (3) ___ you of our sad news, but next week will be the last week of this daily newspaper. We would like to thank all the people who have enjoyed our newspaper over the years, but it is time for a change. Unfortunately, we do not have a lot of money, and it is too expensive to (4) ___ so many (5) ___ of our newspaper every day. Many (6) ___ who have worked with us for years have decided to stop working, but younger ones will try to find other jobs in (7) ___.

We hope that you will use other news sites online, where you can watch video clips and read the news every day. It's fast and easy – you just need to (8) ___ on a page and the news is there. Again, thank you for all the years that you have been with us.

	A	B	C
1	**A** copies	**B** editor	**C** print
2	**A** readers	**B** copies	**C** the media
3	**A** inform	**B** print	**C** click
4	**A** copy	**B** inform	**C** print
5	**A** readers	**B** copies	**C** editors
6	**A** journalists	**B** readers	**C** inform
7	**A** editor	**B** the media	**C** print
8	**A** copy	**B** inform	**C** click

4 Choose the correct word.

1 How many **journalists / copies** work for this paper?
2 If you want to write that story, talk to the **editor / print** first.
3 Look! That local newspaper has **printed / informed** an article about our school!
4 The magazine sells more than 40,000 **copies / editors** every week.
5 Watch, if you want to open this page online, just **copy / click** here.
6 If you love photography and writing maybe you should try to get a job in **the media / journalists**.
7 This website was built to **inform / copy** readers about sports news.
8 The online news site has more than 50,000 **copies / readers** a day.

Grammar 1

G

Relative clauses

Look again at *Grammar database 27* on page 154 before doing these exercises.

1 Choose the correct word.

1 I love magazines **that / who** are about fashion.
2 Do you ever visit websites **where / whose** you can watch the news?
3 There are many readers **who / whose** do not like reading the news online.
4 A friend of mine **whose / which** son works in the media says many newspapers are disappearing.
5 The newspaper **who / which** my dad works for has a very good website.
6 A newspaper **that / who** started over hundred years ago finally closed last week.
7 The photo **that / where** your daughter sent to the newspaper was amazing.
8 People **who / where** read news online are usually good with computers.

2 Read the sentences with relative clauses and choose the option, a or b, which is true.

1 That's the man whose daughter is a famous journalist.
 a The man is a famous journalist.
 b The daughter is a famous journalist.
2 She's the reader who wrote weekly letters to the editor.
 a The woman wrote the letters.
 b The editor wrote the letters.
3 The journalists who work for that new online newspaper are very happy.
 a The site has happy news.
 b The journalists are happy.
4 The old red building where our local newspaper is printed is next to our school.
 a The newspaper is printed next to our school.
 b Our school is an old red building.
5 The thunderstorm that the journalist is talking about destroyed two houses.
 a Two houses were destroyed by the thunderstorm.
 b The journalist destroyed two houses.
6 That's the new magazine that my cousin works for.
 a My cousin has got a new magazine.
 b My cousin has got a job for a magazine.

3 Complete the sentences with relative clauses. In some sentences, two different words are possible.

1 It was our teacher *who / that* started the school website.
2 I know great sites ________ have news for teenagers.
3 Do you know a shop ________ I can buy a computer magazine?
4 Isn't he the boy ________ was on TV last night?
5 Is that the girl ________ father owns the radio station?
6 That's the office ________ my dad used to work.
7 Look! This is the new iPad™ ________ I'd like to buy.
8 That is the woman ________ son won the photography competition.

Wordpower!

1 Make sentences using the correct form of the word in bold.

1 I don't enjoy being on TV. I feel __________ in front of the camera. **comfortable**
2 I'm sorry, but I'm __________ to use this computer. Can you help me? **able**
3 Listen to this man shouting at the journalist on TV. Why is he so __________ to him? **polite**
4 Don't choose a career in the media if you think you will be __________. **happy**
5 Wow! That video clip about the earthquake was __________. **believable**
6 I'm still __________ about what job I'd like to have when I'm older. **sure**
7 Our editor is __________ to work with. He changes his mind all the time! **possible**
8 You don't have to wear anything special for the TV interview. It's very __________. **formal**
9 Don't wear those jeans! They're so __________! **fashionable**
10 This website won't open at all. I think it's been __________ for months. **active**

2 Match to make sentences.

1 Some readers were unhappy ___
2 Many journalists feel uncertain ___
3 It is impossible to know ___
4 Some famous people are impolite ___
5 The photos of the earthquake ___
6 My uncle is incapable of ___
7 The colours of the video were imperfect ___
8 The editor was unable to ___

a if newspapers always print the truth.
b so the news site didn't show the clip.
c were unbelievable.
d tell us how many copies were printed each week.
e when the local newspaper went online.
f when they are interviewed on TV.
g about the future of their jobs.
h reading the news online.

Listening

14

1 KET Listen to a radio programme about different news websites and complete the information.

1 Every week the man talks about __________ new websites that he likes.
2 On the first website, the news is about __________ games.
3 You can play games free for __________ minutes.
4 The man's favourite game was called *Mystery* __________.
5 The game is good for children aged __________ or older.
6 On the second website, the news is about different __________.
7 This week, the second website had news from __________.
8 On the third site, the news is about __________ events around the world.
9 The man's favourite sports events on this site was the __________ climbing.
10 You can watch a film on the site called *Climb to the* __________.

Grammar 2

G

Question tags

Look again at *Grammar database 28* on page 154 before doing these exercises.

1 Choose the correct question tag.

1 You saw the news about the earthquake, **haven't you / didn't you**?
2 Peter's new video camera is fantastic, **doesn't it / isn't it**?
3 There are lots of great jobs in the media, **aren't there / isn't there**?
4 That man hasn't been a journalist for very many years, **hasn't he / has he**?
5 You're very comfortable in front of a camera, **aren't you / won't you**?
6 That radio station doesn't play good music, **does it / doesn't it**?
7 Eva is working for a fashion magazine, **doesn't she / isn't she**?
8 Your brother will be a very good writer one day, **won't he / isn't he**?

2 Write a question tag in each gap. Then read the questions again and match them to the answers (a–h).

1 'You want to work in the media, ___________?' h
2 'That news video about the thunderstorm was amazing, ___________?' ___
3 'This TV programme isn't very interesting, ___________?' ___
4 'Your brother works at that radio station, ___________?' ___
5 'Stephen can speak Russian, ___________?' ___
6 'Those iPads™ are amazing, ___________?' ___
7 'You started a news blog last year, ___________?' ___
8 'Your mum has interviewed lots of celebrities ___________?' ___

a 'Yes, and I know a website where they don't cost so much!'
b 'Yes, and did you see the lightning that hit the houses! Pretty amazing, wasn't it?'
c 'Yes, and some of them weren't very polite when she asked them questions!'
d 'Yes, he loves it. He chooses the music that they play.'
e 'I agree. Let's watch a video that we both like.'
f 'That's right, and now I have more than 2,000 readers!'
g 'Yes, and he can write it well too.'
h 'Yes, I would love to be a journalist one day.'

✓ Quick check

3 Put a line through the incorrect sentence.

1 That's the man who works for the TV station. / That's the man whose works for the TV station.
2 The city that the earthquake happened is being rebuilt. / The city where the earthquake happened is being rebuilt.
3 I like that website which showed videos of skateboarding. / I like that website showed videos of skateboarding.
4 You go online every day, don't you? / You go online every day, aren't you?
5 He's a very capable writer, doesn't he? / He's a very capable writer, isn't he?
6 You would like a career in the media, wouldn't you? / You would like a career in the media, can't you?
7 Mike has been on TV before, didn't he? / Mike has been on TV before, hasn't he?
8 The journalist looked unhappy during the interview, didn't she? / The journalist looked unhappy during the interview, wasn't she?

Writing

1 Here are five opening questions for magazine articles. Match the opening question of each article with a title (a–e).

1 Everyone likes to know what's happening around the world, don't they? ___
2 We all enjoy a great film, don't we? ___
3 We all love to eat good food, don't we? ___
4 You always want to see your favourite team play, don't you? ___
5 We all like to wear nice clothes, don't we? ___

a Restaurants of the future!
b Spectators are online!
c International news online!
d Shopping online!
e Cinemas are changing!

2 Read the magazine article and match each paragraph with a statement.

Cinemas of the future

(1) We all love watching a good film, don't we? For years, going to the cinema has been one of the most popular things to do in our free time. The fun we have meeting friends before the film, laughing, crying or being scared during the film – and then talking about the story when the film has finished. But will the cinema always be like this? No, of course not! With technology, it will be more exciting and more fun.

(2) During the last hundred years the cinema has changed a lot. At first, films had no sound and the picture was black and white. The words that the actors said were written on the screen and sometimes a pianist played music in the cinema, especially during the frightening moments. Then with technology, films included sound, colour and even drawings that moved (called cartoons).

(3) Today, many films include real actors and cartoon creatures at the same time. Computers are used to do this and it is amazing to watch! Nothing is impossible to do in a film today! One of the most important changes in films right now is the idea of 3D films. Films which are made in 3D are the closest thing to real life. It feels like we can really touch the actors!

(4) So what can we expect from cinemas of the future? Will we be able to feel what is happening in the film? If there is an earthquake in the film, will we use technology to shake the people in the cinema? If there are flowers in the film, will we be able to really smell those flowers? It would be wonderful if we can really go into the film, wouldn't it? Some experts say this might be the cinema experience of the future. Amazing idea, isn't it?

1 Paragraph 1 ___
2 Paragraph 2 ___
3 Paragraph 3 ___
4 Paragraph 4 ___

a describes how the cinema might be in the future.
b gives information about films that we see today.
c gives general information about going to the cinema.
d talks about the history of the cinema.

Check your progress! | Units 13–14

1 Choose the correct word.

1 If you want, I can **make / get** my mum to drive us.
2 Watch out! I'm **right / opposite** behind you!
3 Have you **made / done** any plans for your holidays?
4 I'm **doing / taking** the bus to Portsmouth later today.
5 I know tests are difficult, but just **make / do** your best.
6 Enjoy yourself at the party and **have / make** a great time!

6 marks

2 Read the text and for each question, choose the correct answer, A, B or C.

Most newspapers and other forms of the (7) ___ are available online these days. It's become a popular choice for reading the news. (8) ___ are choosing to read the news online because it's easier than buying a (9) ___ of the paper from a newsagent's. It may be (10) ___ , but some newspaper companies don't (11) ___ newspapers on paper any more. They are (12) ___ to make money from selling newspapers at a newsagent's.

	A	B	C
7	magazines	media	programmes
8	Readers	Editors	Journalists
9	form	copy	text
10	unbelievable	unsure	imperfect
11	inform	click	print
12	unfashionable	unable	incapable

6 marks

3 Write a word from the box in each gap to complete the text.

at • by • for • in • on • since

Nicole: Daniel, do you want to meet (13) __________ Thursday?
Daniel: Sure. Let's meet (14) __________ the town centre, if that's OK with you.
Nicole: OK, I live close to there. I'll go (15) __________ bike.
Daniel: Oh, I didn't know you'd got a bike.
Nicole: Yes, I've had it (16) __________ July. It's nice. I'll show it to you.
Daniel: Great. So, do you want to meet (17) __________ the cinema?
Nicole: OK. We can see *The Incredibles*. It's been on (18) __________ two weeks and I haven't seen it yet.
Daniel: Great. I'll see you then!

6 marks

4 Match to make sentences.

19 That's the company where ___
20 This is where you work, ___
21 A company whose ___
22 You've got that magazine, ___
23 A journalist who ___
24 The programme isn't on tonight, ___
25 That's the magazine which ___

a isn't it?
b writes well is popular.
c is it?
d Julie works.
e haven't you?
f has got articles on photography.
g workers are happy is a good company.

7 marks

Total: ___ / 25 marks

Check your progress! | Units 1–14

1 Read the sentences and for each question, choose the correct answer, A, B or C.

1 What time do you usually ___ home after school?

A wake up **B** get up **C** get back

2 Last year I ___ a music club and I love hanging out with the other members.

A joined **B** collected **C** played

3 'What were you doing when you heard this ___ scream?' asked the detective.

A unfortunately **B** distance **C** strange

4 I sent the invitations to everyone last week and I've had about 20 ___ .

A popular **B** replies **C** order

5 Tomorrow morning, our class is going to ___ an art gallery.

A find out **B** guide **C** visit

6 My brother is going to a new school this year and he's really ___ about it.

A secondary **B** nervous **C** primary

7 Do you know when that office ___ was built?

A centre **B** block **C** hall

8 It's so cold! The ___ has fallen very quickly since this morning, hasn't it?

A temperature **B** ground **C** flash

9 We've bought lots of ___ for the party and I'm going to make a birthday cake.

A tasty **B** ingredients **C** snacks

10 That guy with the short dark hair is very ___ , isn't he? He talks to everyone!

A sociable **B** generous **C** shy

11 My mum told me to tidy up my room and to ___ my jacket and shirt.

A hang up **B** put on **C** tie up

12 If you want to ___ , why don't you join a gym?

A take part **B** take up **C** get fit

13 Jim, could you ___ me a big favour and help me organise the party?

A make **B** do **C** take

14 That ___ always writes fantastic articles.

A journalist **B** media **C** copy

14 marks

2 Put the verbs into the correct form to complete the letter.

Dear Sir,

I am writing to you because I would like (15) ___________ (**take part**) in the summer school for young musicians in London this year. Here is the information about me that you asked for.

My name is Andreas, I am 16 years old and I (16) ___________ (**live**) in Madrid. I can speak Spanish, French and English. I (17) ___________ (**play**) the guitar and the violin since I was eight years old. Last year, I decided (18) ___________ (**learn**) the piano. If I (19) ___________ (**have**) enough free time next year, I will take up the drums too. Unfortunately, our house is not close to a music school. If I (20) ___________ (**live**) nearer a music school, I would like to study singing too.

Please let me know if you would like more information about my music studies.

I look forward to your reply.

Kind regards,

Andreas Black

6 marks

3 Choose the correct word.

21 Come to the party! I'm sure you will **to enjoy / enjoy** yourself there.

22 We have to play indoors today **because / so** it's too cold outside.

23 Your clothes are more fashionable **than / that** mine.

24 I am a much **worse / worst** dancer than you! Watch me!

25 That is the editor **who / whose** newspaper printed wrong information about our school.

5 marks

Total: ___ / 25 marks

Answer key

Unit 1
The Youth of Today!

Reading

Exercise 1
1 B 2 C 3 C 4 B 5 B

Wordpower!

Exercise 2
1 blog
2 drive
3 check
4 chat
5 choose
6 do
7 uniform
8 ring

Exercise 3
1 rings
2 uniform
3 choose
4 check
5 send
6 drives
7 do
8 chat
9 blog
10 spend

Grammar 1

Exercise 1
1 brings
2 do
3 live
4 spend
5 Do you
6 don't
7 Does
8 get

Exercise 2
1 gets
2 stay
3 brings
4 eat
5 spends
6 watch
7 does
8 goes

Exercise 3
2 Does Beth have breakfast every morning?
3 Do they ride bikes to school?
4 Do the students read your blog?
5 Do they do their homework every night?
6 Does Henry go to bed at midnight?
7 Do you wear a uniform to school every day?
8 Do Tom and Erin go to the cinema at the weekends?

Exercise 4
1 I don't
2 he does
3 you do
4 he doesn't
5 they don't
6 I do

Wordpower!

Exercise 1
1 come home
2 stop a light
3 start a light
4 stop sleeping
5 leave the house
6 leave your bed

Exercise 2
1 wake up
2 go out
3 turn on
4 turn off
5 get up
6 get back

Listening

Exercise 1
1 f 2 a 3 b 4 c 5 e

Grammar 2

Exercise 1
1 are playing
2 drives
3 go
4 am not doing
5 Are you chatting
6 do your parents usually do
7 are you doing
8 aren't having

Exercise 2
1 is winning
2 isn't going
3 is writing
4 are walking
5 is playing
6 am reading

Exercise 3
1 usually gets
2 always has
3 doesn't leave
4 is getting
5 always goes
6 are playing
7 usually wins
8 isn't winning
9 is chatting
10 spends
11 are talking
12 is telling

Quick check

Exercise 4
1 yes
2 no
3 I read at night.
4 I'm eating now.
5 no
6 yes

Writing

Exercise 1
1 C 2 B 3 C 4 A

Exercise 2
1 B 2 B

Unit 2
Having Fun!

Reading

Exercise 1
1 b 2 c 3 d 4 a

Wordpower!

Exercise 2

1 B 2 A 3 A 4 C 5 B 6 C 7 B 8 B

Exercise 3

1 free time
2 video games
3 hang out
4 joined
5 beginner
6 hobby
7 collect
8 member

Grammar 1

Exercise 1

1 went
2 did / eat
3 took
4 Did / do
5 bought
6 didn't know
7 did / get
8 wasn't

Exercise 2

1 had
2 went
3 were
4 took
5 bought
6 sent

Exercise 3

1 Did / b
2 Did / e
3 Was / a
4 Did / f
5 Were / d
6 Did / c

Wordpower!

Exercise 1

1 cyclist
2 photographer
3 guitarist
4 player
5 pianist
6 windsurfer
7 gamers
8 collector

Exercise 2

1 collect
2 violinist
3 skater
4 players
5 pianist
6 surfer
7 golfer
8 painter

Listening

Exercise 1

1 c 2 d 3 a 4 b

Exercise 2

1 video games
2 guitarist
3 skateboarding
4 sports
5 model aeroplane club
6 video games
7 dancers
8 they are

Grammar 2

Exercise 1

1 told
2 bought
3 found
4 spent
5 drew
6 paid
7 built
8 said
9 ate
10 won

Exercise 2

1 B 2 A 3 C 4 A 5 B 6 B

Exercise 3

1 spent
2 taught
3 left
4 brought
5 told
6 hit

Quick check

Exercise 4

1 I joined a new club last week.
2 My family didn't go to the cinema last night.
3 Did you write to your cousin?
4 My friends had fun last night.
5 My sister bought a new skateboard yesterday.

Writing

Exercise 1

1 I wasn't home last night.
2 The shops weren't open yesterday.
3 We didn't have much free time today.
4 My favourite teacher wasn't at school on Tuesday.
5 I didn't send the email to you last week.
6 My dad didn't collect things when he was young.

Exercise 2

1 It's
2 There's
3 wasn't
4 didn't
5 I've

Exercise 3

1 C 2 B 3 A 4 A

Check your progress! | Units 1–2

Exercise 1

1 B 2 A 3 C 4 A 5 C 6 B 7 C 8 C 9 B

Exercise 2

10 do
11 enjoys
12 is reading
13 doesn't like
14 plays
15 isn't taking
16 sit
17 helps

Exercise 3

18 were
19 took
20 Did you go
21 played
22 brought
23 didn't write
24 built
25 spent

Unit 3
Tell me a Story!

Reading

Exercise 1

1 B 2 A 3 C 4 A 5 A 6 A 7 A 8 B

Wordpower!

Exercise 2

1 disappear
2 childhood
3 strange
4 worried
5 distance
6 terrible
7 notice
8 unfortunately

Exercise 3

1 childhood
2 strange
3 terrible
4 worried
5 unfortunately
6 notice
7 distance
8 disappeared

Exercise 4

1 distance
2 worried
3 notice
4 childhood
5 disappeared
6 strange
7 unfortunately

Grammar 1

Exercise 1

1 heard
2 was reading
3 arrived
4 jumped
5 was doing
6 came
7 was writing
8 was running

Exercise 2

1 was doing
2 was looking
3 decided
4 was walking
5 arrived
6 walked
7 opened
8 was watching

Exercise 3

1 B 2 C 3 A 4 C 5 C 6 A 7 B 8 C

Wordpower!

Exercise 1

1 at
2 at
3 about
4 about
5 for
6 to

Exercise 2

1 for
2 about
3 at
4 at
5 about
6 with
7 for
8 to

Listening

Exercise 1

1 watching TV
2 joke
3 kitchen
4 turned on
5 terrible
6 cinema

Grammar 2

Exercise 1

1 to read
2 visiting
3 looking
4 to go
5 to close
6 staying

Exercise 2

2 Don't open the door!
3 Do your homework!
4 Read the story again!
5 Don't talk in class!
6 Turn off the lights!

Exercise 3

1 B 2 C 3 B 4 C 5 A 6 B 7 C 8 B

Quick check

Exercise 4

1 yes 2 no 3 both 4 no 5 yes
6 He was working at 1pm.

Writing

Exercise 1

1 d 2 e 3 c 4 b 5 a

Exercise 2

1 C 2 C 3 C

Unit 4
Let's Celebrate!

Reading

Exercise 1

1 c 2 d 3 b 4 a

Wordpower!

Exercise 2

1 C 2 B 3 A 4 B 5 A 6 B 7 C 8 B

Exercise 3

1 outdoors
2 indoors
3 popular
4 cheap
5 order
6 tidy up
7 arrive
8 reply

Grammar 1

Exercise 1

1 C 2 B 3 C 4 B 5 C 6 A

Exercise 2

1 haven't
2 yet
3 already
4 Have
5 hasn't
6 just
7 ago
8 has

Wordpower!

Exercise 1

1 interesting
2 interested
3 amazing
4 frightening

Exercise 2

1 interesting
2 frightening
3 amazing
4 excited
5 interested
6 amazed

Listening

Exercise 1

1 A 2 C 3 B 4 A 5 B

Grammar 2

Exercise 1

2 have ridden
3 hasn't seen
4 have eaten
5 hasn't been
6 haven't seen

Exercise 2

2 Have ... ridden Yes, they have.
3 Has ... ridden No, she hasn't.
4 Has ... eaten Yes, he has.
5 Has ... been No, he hasn't.
6 Has ... eaten No, she hasn't.
7 Has ... been Yes, she has.

Quick check

Exercise 3
1 I saw Kevin at the party last night.
2 I haven't tidied my room yet.
3 No, I haven't.
4 My dad has just bought a new car!
5 I haven't had dinner yet.

Writing

Exercise 1
2 F 3 F 4 NF 5 F 6 NF

Exercise 2
1 B 2 C 3 B 4 B 5 A 6 A

Check your progress! | Units 3–4

Exercise 1
1 B 2 B 3 C 4 C 5 A 6 C 7 B 8 A

Exercise 2
9 at 10 to 11 about 12 for 13 at

Exercise 3
14 were having / heard
15 was watching / told
16 were you doing / didn't answer
17 was tidying up / found
18 to invite
19 reading

Exercise 4
20 Have / haven't
21 Has / has
22 haven't
23 Don't
24 Tidy
25 tell

Unit 5
Off we Go!

Reading

Exercise 1
1 magazine
2 adults

Exercise 2
1 eight
2 history
3 school trips
4 young kids
5 famous people

Wordpower!

Exercise 3
1 B 2 C 3 A 4 B 5 C 6 B

Exercise 4
1 trip
2 visit
3 organise
4 view
5 find
6 clear
7 past
8 enjoy
9 experience

Grammar 1

Exercise 1
1 B 2 A 3 B 4 B 5 A 6 C

Exercise 2
1 going
2 won't
3 are
4 be
5 will
6 am
7 aren't
8 have

Exercise 3
1 h 2 c 3 f 4 b 5 g 6 e 7 a 8 d

Wordpower!

Exercise 1
1 sun cream
2 guide book
3 driving licence
4 tour guide
5 school trip
6 train ticket
7 guided tour
8 credit card

Exercise 2
1 school trip
2 guided tour
3 tour guide
4 guide book
5 sun cream
6 credit card
7 driving licence
8 train ticket

Listening

Exercise 1
1 Broad
2 48 pounds
3 01273 840 322
4 (the) beach
5 Monday(s)

Grammar 2

Exercise 1
1 land
2 get
3 are staying
4 leaves
5 are
6 arrive

Exercise 2
1 does
2 leaves
3 are
4 after
5 staying
6 as

Exercise 3
1 B 2 C 3 B 4 B 5 C 6 B 7 B 8 C 9 C 10 A

Quick check

Exercise 4
1 yes
2 yes
3 both
4 yes
5 yes
6 We're staying for three days.

Writing

Exercise 1
1 B 2 B 3 C

Exercise 2
1 d 2 c 3 a

Unit 6
Doing it Right!

Reading

Exercise 1
1 B 2 A 3 A 4 C 5 C 6 A

Wordpower!

Exercise 2

1 lonely 2 interests 3 group 4 nervous 5 primary 6 make 7 touch 8 secondary

Exercise 3

1 primary 2 lonely 3 secondary 4 make 5 nervous 6 interests 7 group 8 touch

Exercise 4

1 interest 2 group 3 school 4 touch 5 lonely 6 make 7 nervous 8 primary

Grammar 1

Exercise 1

1 A 2 B 3 A 4 C 5 A 6 C 7 B 8 A

Exercise 2

1 you should 2 I don't 3 you can 4 she does 5 you can 6 he doesn't 7 I do 8 you shouldn't

Exercise 3

1 b 2 a 3 b 4 b

Wordpower!

Exercise 1

1 with 2 for 3 about 4 to 5 at 6 on

Exercise 2

1 f 2 c 3 b 4 a 5 d 6 e

Listening

Exercise 1

1 A 2 B 3 A 4 C 5 B 6 C

Grammar 2

Exercise 1

1 You could be very famous one day.
2 I might join the video club this year.
3 This film should be very good.
4 We might have a maths test tomorrow.
5 I may be late for school tomorrow.
6 It may rain later today.

Exercise 2

1 A 2 B 3 C 4 A 5 B 6 A 7 B 8 C 9 B 10 A

Quick check

Exercise 3

1 You should do all your homework.
2 I don't have to go to school today.
3 You shouldn't be nervous.
4 I might have an exam today.
5 Our teacher may be away today.

Writing

Exercise 1

2 NF 3 F 4 NF

Exercise 2

1 true 2 true 3 false 4 three 5 rules 6 hobbies 7 buildings 8 friendly

Check your progress! | Units 5–6

Exercise 1

1 B 2 C 3 C 4 C 5 A 6 A 7 C 8 C 9 B 10 B 11 A

Exercise 2

12 going 13 is 14 will 15 won't 16 be 17 are

Exercise 3

18 have to 19 mustn't 20 should 21 can 22 might 23 can 24 won't 25 could

Unit 7

Make it, Build it!

Reading

Exercise 1

1 B 2 C 3 B 4 C 5 C

Wordpower!

Exercise 2

1 calculator 2 mobile 3 city 4 genius 5 battery 6 tower

Exercise 3

1 C 2 C 3 A 4 C 5 B 6 B 7 A 8 B

Exercise 4

1 invented 2 genius 3 designed 4 battery 5 found 6 calculator 7 cities 8 towers 9 built

Grammar 1

Exercise 1

1 was 2 were 3 Pompeii discovered 4 is 5 are 6 Is

Exercise 2

1 was taken 2 were carried 3 were built 4 are found 5 Is ... cleaned 6 wasn't bought

Exercise 3

1 wasn't 2 was 3 weren't 4 are 5 is 6 isn't

Exercise 4

1 is 2 are 3 is 4 weren't 5 was 6 wasn't

Wordpower!

Exercise 1

1 post office	4 microwave oven	7 office block
2 town hall	5 digital clock	8 art gallery
3 washing machine	6 MP3 player	

Exercise 2

1 e 2 h 3 b 4 g 5 a 6 d 7 f 8 c

Listening

Exercise 1

1 adults 2 1997 3 25 4 USA 5 1 / one

Grammar 2

Exercise 1

1 B 2 A 3 C 4 A 5 B 6 A 7 A 8 C 9 A

Exercise 2

1 The White House was finished in 1800.
2 Telephones were invented in 1876.
3 The first DVD was sold in 1996.
4 Paper was developed in the year 105.

Exercise 3

1 The pyramids were built by the Egyptians.
2 The Statue of Liberty was designed by a Frenchman.
3 Terrific games consoles are made by Nintendo.
4 The MP3 player is often used by young people.
5 The old house was destroyed by a terrible storm.
6 The Great Wall of China is visited by millions of people.

Quick check

Exercise 4

1 no	3 Computers are made here.	5 no
2 yes	4 no	6 both

Writing

Exercise 1

1 bedroom	4 bird sounds
2 can't sleep at night	5 stars
3 inside the clock	6 many shops

Exercise 2

1 d 2 b 3 f 4 a 5 e 6 c

Unit 8
Weird World!

Reading

Exercise 1

1 c 2 d 3 e 4 b 5 a

Wordpower!

Exercise 2

1 temperature	4 ground	7 thunderstorm
2 lake	5 common	8 creatures
3 flash	6 weird	

Exercise 3

1 flash	5 creature
2 lake	6 ground
3 thunderstorm	7 weird
4 temperature	8 common

Exercise 4

1 e 2 d 3 g 4 h 5 f 6 c 7 a 8 b

Grammar 1

Exercise 1

1 an	3 The	5 The	7 –
2 the	4 –	6 a	8 the

Exercise 2

1 C	4 B	7 C	10 C
2 C	5 A	8 A	11 B
3 A	6 A	9 A	12 A

Exercise 3

1 b 2 a 3 b 4 a

Wordpower!

Exercise 1

1 windy	4 foggy	7 cloudy
2 sunny	5 snowy	8 stormy
3 misty	6 frosty	9 rainy

Exercise 2

1 sun	4 foggy	7 snowy
2 misty	5 rainy	8 windy
3 storm	6 cloud	9 frost

Listening

Exercise 1

1 C 2 B 3 A 4 C

Exercise 2

1 T 2 F 3 T 4 F

Grammar 2

Exercise 1

1 UC	4 UC	7 C	10 UC
2 UC	5 C	8 C	11 UC
3 C	6 UC	9 C	12 C

Exercise 2

1 –	3 some	5 the	7 the
2 a	4 some	6 –	8 some

Quick check

Exercise 3

1 Do you like the little lake in our town?
2 I don't like earthquakes!
3 The frogs in that river make weird noises.
4 I think the information in this book about storms is wrong.
5 Have you ever seen lightning?

Writing

Exercise 1

2 A 3 A 4 NA 5 NA 6 A

Exercise 2

1 amazing 2 beautiful 3 big 4 wonderful

Exercise 3

1 B 2 A 3 C 4 B

Check your progress! | Units 7–8

Exercise 1

1 B 2 A 3 C 4 A 5 A 6 C 7 B 8 B 9 C

Exercise 2

10 is called
11 was given
12 are built
13 was designed
14 were destroyed
15 is visited
16 has been stolen
17 are told
18 were invented

Exercise 3

19 –
20 the
21 –
22 the
23 some
24 The
25 –

Unit 9
Want any more?

Reading

Exercise 1

1 G 2 B 3 E 4 A 5 D 6 C

Wordpower!

Exercise 2

1 cut
2 frozen
3 snack
4 fizzy
5 fry
6 tasty
7 ingredients
8 fresh
9 sugar-free
10 margarine

Exercise 3

1 frozen
2 fresh
3 fry
4 cut
5 snack
6 ingredients
7 margarine
8 tasty
9 fizzy
10 sugar-free

Grammar 1

Exercise 1

1 c 2 d 3 f 4 e 5 a 6 b

Exercise 2

1 A 2 B 3 C 4 A 5 B 6 A

Exercise 3

1 lot
2 few
3 lots
4 many
5 much
6 little

Exercise 4

1 a
2 of
3 not
4 a
5 of
6 a

Wordpower!

Exercise 1

1 C 2 A 3 B 4 C 5 B 6 C 7 A 8 C

Exercise 2

1 from
2 look
3 like
4 taste
5 come
6 for
7 pay
8 go

Listening

Exercise 1

1 A 2 B 3 B 4 C 5 C 6 B

Grammar 2

Exercise 2

1 where
2 and
3 but
4 because
5 when
6 or

Exercise 3

1 because
2 but
3 when
4 and
5 where
6 or

Exercise 4

1 because
2 where
3 and
4 because
5 or
6 when
7 when
8 or
9 or
10 when
11 and

Quick check

Exercise 4

1 yes
2 no
3 both
4 no
5 yes
6 I like tomatoes because they're tasty.

Writing

Exercise 1

1 C 2 E 3 D 4 A 5 F 6 B

Exercise 2

1 C 2 B 3 A 4 C

Unit 10
All Sorts of People!

Reading

Exercise 1

1 e 2 f 3 a 4 b 5 d 6 c

Wordpower!

Exercise 2

1 guy
2 shy
3 polite
4 artistic
5 sociable
6 handsome
7 trendy
8 generous

Exercise 3

1 B 2 A 3 C 4 A 5 C 6 B 7 C 8 B

Exercise 4

1 d 2 e 3 g 4 f 5 c 6 a 7 h 8 b

Grammar 1

Exercise 1

1 the	4 a	7 a	10 the
2 a	5 the	8 a	11 the
3 an	6 –	9 –	12 a

Exercise 2

1 b 2 a 3 b 4 a 5 a 6 b 7 a 8 b

Wordpower!

Exercise 1

1 forgetful	4 careful	7 wonderful
2 energetic	5 helpful	8 thoughtful
3 pessimistic	6 athletic	

Exercise 2

1 e 2 c 3 a 4 b 5 d 6 f

Listening

Exercise 1

1 C 2 A 3 B 4 C

Grammar 2

Exercise 1

1 loudly	4 short blonde	7 long red
2 funny little	5 carefully	8 well
3 late	6 hard	

Exercise 2

1 suddenly	4 happily	7 finally
2 lovely	5 completely	8 weekly
3 totally	6 beautifully	

Exercise 3

2 Sue sings beautifully.
3 Tim dances badly.
4 Olga cooks well.
5 Paul learns quickly.
6 Mike works hard.

Quick check

Exercise 4

1 Can you speak Spanish?
2 My mum's a doctor.
3 Do you like my new red hat?
4 My brother's got short black hair.
5 You can draw very well.
6 My dad drives carefully.

Writing

Exercise 1

1 cheerful	3 short black
2 tall	4 happy, optimistic

Exercise 2

1 well	3 fast
2 beautifully	4 nicely

Exercise 3

1 C 2 A 3 A

Check your progress! | Units 9–10

Exercise 1

1 B	3 C	5 B	7 A	9 A
2 B	4 A	6 C	8 B	10 B

Exercise 2

11 few	14 lot	17 many
12 little	15 but	18 and
13 lots	16 of	

Exercise 3

19 a	22 carefully	24 silly little red
20 –	23 –	25 the
21 lovely long blue		

Unit 11
Looking Good!

Reading

Exercise 1

1 T 2 F 3 T

Exercise 2

1 comfortable	3 interesting	5 terrible
2 casual	4 short	

Wordpower!

Exercise 3

clothes: casual, colourful, dyed, plain, skinny, tight
hair: colourful, curly, dyed, spiky

Exercise 4

1 C 2 B 3 C 4 A 5 C 6 C 7 C 8 B

Exercise 5

1 casual	4 tight	7 curly
2 plain	5 skinny	8 dyed
3 colourful	6 spiky	

Grammar 1

Exercise 1

1 longer	3 curlier	5 better
2 wider	4 more colourful	6 worse

Exercise 2

1 taller	3 than	5 more casual
2 skinnier	4 fashionable	6 faster

Exercise 3

2 My mum's hair is straighter than mine.
3 Martin's trousers are not tighter than Kevin's.
4 His suit is more formal than Fred's t-shirt and jeans.
5 Her earrings are bigger than Jill's.
6 This dress is longer than my other one.
7 Cindy is worse than her sister at getting dressed.
8 Mike is better than Ralph at shopping.

Exercise 4

1 older than	3 cooler than	5 more important
2 taller than	4 longer than	6 happier

Wordpower!

Exercise 1

1 take	3 dress	5 leave	7 put
2 hang	4 have	6 do	8 try

Exercise 2

1 up 2 on 3 on 4 on 5 up 6 off 7 on 8 up

Listening

Exercise 1

1 green	3 yellow	5 blue
2 comfortable	4 larger	6 small

Grammar 2

Exercise 1

1 the most stylish	4 the worst
2 the best	5 the ugliest
3 the most fashionable	6 the cheapest

Exercise 2

2 That's the loveliest dress I've ever seen.
3 This is the largest clothing shop in town.
4 These are the most comfortable shoes that we sell.
5 This isn't the best costume for the party.

Exercise 3

1 C	3 B	5 C	7 B	9 C	11 C
2 C	4 B	6 A	8 A	10 B	

Quick check

Exercise 4

1 yes	4 both
2 She's shorter than Martin.	5 both
3 more than two things	

Writing

Exercise 1

1 Models 2 the office 3 shopping centre

Exercise 2

1 C 2 B 3 C 4 C 5 A

Unit 12
It's a Goal!

Reading

Exercise 1

1 d 2 c 3 e 4 b 5 a

Wordpower!

Exercise 2

1 train	4 get fit	7 match
2 spectators	5 stadium	8 take part
3 final	6 take up	

Exercise 3

1 A 2 B 3 C 4 A 5 A 6 C 7 A 8 C

Grammar 1

Exercise 1

1 FC	3 ZC	5 ZC	7 FC
2 FC	4 FC	6 FC	8 ZC

Exercise 2

1 a 2 a 3 b 4 a 5 b

Exercise 3

1 I join	3 I'll be	5 I'll do
2 I spend	4 I am	6 I take up

Wordpower!

Exercise 1

1 go	4 play	7 win
2 score	5 do	8 learn
3 beat	6 train	

Exercise 2

1 been	4 beat	7 plays
2 learn	5 scored	8 win
3 train	6 does	

Listening

Exercise 1

1 Milton	3 295	5 0219 7345
2 15 pounds	4 6am	

Exercise 2

1 b 2 a 3 a 4 b

Grammar 2

Exercise 1

2 had / would join	6 were / would go
3 trained / would get fit	7 had / would build
4 lived / would take up	8 wore / wouldn't hurt
5 met / would feel	

Exercise 2

1 did	4 would	7 was
2 would	5 was	8 would
3 went	6 wouldn't	

Quick check

Exercise 3

1 If you want to be a professional footballer, you will have to practise a lot.
2 Today is your birthday so if you tell me what you want to do, I'll do it.
3 If I had more money, I would take up windsurfing.
4 If you did sports more often, you would feel healthier.
5 If there was a gym near my house, I would work out very often.

Writing

Exercise 1

1 are used
2 are worn
3 is needed
4 is used
5 is played

Exercise 2

1 A 2 B 3 B

Check your progress! | Units 11–12

Exercise 1

1 B 2 A 3 C 4 A 5 A 6 C 7 B 8 C

Exercise 2

9 fastest
10 older
11 faster
12 best
13 tallest
14 better
15 laziest
16 worst

Exercise 3

17 had
18 knew
19 had
20 buy
21 knew
22 are
23 would / could take up
24 lived
25 could

Unit 13
Right Time, Right Place!

Reading

Exercise 1

1 train stations 2 Europe 3 1800s

Exercise 2

1 A 2 A 3 B 4 B 5 C 6 A 7 A

Wordpower!

Exercise 3

1 c 2 e 3 f 4 g 5 d 6 b 7 a

Exercise 4

1 main
2 above
3 opposite
4 right

Exercise 5

1 got
2 opposite
3 main
4 got
5 on
6 wrong
7 right
8 above

Grammar 1

Exercise 1

1 on
2 for
3 ✓
4 at
5 on
6 for
7 of
8 in
9 ✓
10 on

Exercise 2

1 in
2 by
3 at
4 next
5 near
6 above
7 in front
8 to
9 outside

Exercise 3

1 to
2 in
3 during
4 on
5 into
6 out of
7 above
8 in
9 in
10 behind
11 outside
12 –

Wordpower!

Exercise 1

1 d 2 f 3 b 4 c 5 e 6 a

Exercise 2

1 B 2 C 3 A 4 B 5 B 6 C 7 C 8 B

Listening

Exercise 1

1 A 2 B 3 B 4 C

Grammar 2

Exercise 1

1 for
2 for
3 since
4 for
5 since
6 for

Exercise 2

1 2008
2 for
3 been
4 two
5 has
6 week

Exercise 3

2 Jason's had a pet bird since October.
3 Leslie's been in the kitchen since a quarter past two.
4 Neil's lived in Brighton since 1997.
5 Vicky's had the tickets for weeks now.
6 Blake's been in class for an hour and a half.

Quick check

Exercise 4

1 both
2 We'll go on foot.
3 I'm at home.
4 no
5 no
6 I've been here since 5pm.

Writing

Exercise 1

1 F 2 T 3 T 4 F

Exercise 2

1 d 2 c 3 a 4 e

Unit 14
Words and Pictures!

Reading

Exercise 1

1 d 2 c 3 e 4 a 5 b

Wordpower!

Exercise 2

1 copies
2 print
3 readers
4 inform
5 the media
6 journalist
7 editor
8 click

Exercise 3

1 B 2 A 3 A 4 C 5 B 6 A 7 B 8 C

Exercise 4

1 journalists
2 editor
3 printed
4 copies
5 click
6 the media
7 inform
8 readers

Grammar 1

Exercise 1

1 that
2 where
3 who
4 whose
5 which
6 that
7 that
8 who

Exercise 2

1 b 2 a 3 b 4 a 5 a 6 b

Exercise 3

2 that / which
3 where
4 who / that
5 whose
6 where
7 that / which
8 whose

Wordpower!

Exercise 1

1 uncomfortable
2 unable
3 impolite
4 unhappy
5 unbelievable
6 unsure
7 impossible
8 informal
9 unfashionable
10 inactive

Exercise 2

1 e 2 g 3 a 4 f 5 c 6 h 7 b 8 d

Listening

Exercise 1

1 three
2 video
3 sixty
4 Planet
5 fourteen / 14
6 animals
7 Africa
8 sports
9 mountain
10 *Sky*

Grammar 2

Exercise 1

1 didn't you
2 isn't it
3 aren't there
4 has he
5 aren't you
6 does it
7 isn't she
8 won't he

Exercise 2

1 don't you
2 wasn't it / b
3 is it / e
4 doesn't he / d
5 can't he / g
6 aren't they / a
7 didn't you / f
8 hasn't she / c

Quick check

Exercise 3

1 That's the man who works for the TV station.
2 The city where the earthquake happened is being rebuilt.
3 I like that website which showed videos of skateboarding.
4 You go online every day, don't you?
5 He's a very capable writer, isn't he?
6 You would like a career in the media, wouldn't you?
7 Mike has been on TV before, hasn't he?
8 The journalist looked unhappy during the interview, didn't she?

Writing

Exercise 1

1 c 2 e 3 a 4 b 5 d

Exercise 2

1 c 2 d 3 b 4 a

Check your progress! | Units 13–14

Exercise 1

1 get
2 right
3 made
4 taking
5 do
6 have

Exercise 2

7 B 8 A 9 B 10 A 11 C 12 B

Exercise 3

13 on
14 in
15 by
16 since
17 at
18 for

Exercise 4

19 d
20 a
21 g
22 e
23 b
24 c
25 f

Check your progress! | Units 1–14

Exercise 1

1 C
2 A
3 C
4 B
5 C
6 B
7 B
8 A
9 C
10 A
11 A
12 C
13 B
14 A

Exercise 2

15 to take part
16 live
17 have played
18 to learn
19 have
20 lived

Exercise 3

21 enjoy
22 because
23 than
24 worse
25 whose

Audioscripts

Unit 1 Listening

George: Elizabeth, do you do any afternoon activities?

Elizabeth: Well, George, I have dance lessons every Thursday. That's my favourite day of the week. What about you?

George: I have guitar lessons at the weekend. I like the guitar, but sometimes I don't want to play it. My friends play football in the afternoon at the weekend. But I have guitar lessons then.

Elizabeth: I see. My friend Lacy has got the same problem. She's got piano lessons on Saturday, so she doesn't do things with her friends. The best thing is to do lessons with friends. That's what my friend Fran does. She's got basketball practice with a lot of her friends.

George: Yeah, my friend Kevin is in a chess club. He plays chess with his friends there. Maybe that's a good idea, to play chess.

Elizabeth: Yes, it sounds fun. Good luck!

Unit 2 Listening

Journalist: Hello Elena. So tell me, what club did you join?

Elena: Well, I love video games so I thought about that club, but in the end I joined a different club. I love going to the cinema, and I want to make my own film ... so I joined the cinema club.

Journalist: So, Nick, what club did you join? The skateboarding club?

Nick: Well, I go skateboarding at home all the time, so I wanted to do something different at school. I thought about the music club, but I'm a really bad guitarist. So, in the end I chose the football club! I love sports and can hang out with my friends too.

Journalist: Dan, how about you? Did you join a sports club?

Dan: No. I didn't want to join a sports club at school. I play sports at the weekend anyway, so I wanted to choose a different club. When I was little, I collected model aeroplanes. I love planes! Last year, my sister was in the model aeroplane club and she built a model aeroplane. I liked it a lot. It flew really high. I want to do the same this year!

Journalist: Linda, I know that you like dancing. Did you join the hip hop dance club?

Linda: Yes. I didn't know what to do at first! I thought about the swimming club and I love video games, but finally I chose the hip hop dance club. All my friends are dancers too, so we can hang out together. I was in this club last year and we did a dance show at a big concert. Everybody loved our dance. I asked the teacher and she said we can do the same show again, so I'm really happy!

Unit 3 Listening

Angela: Something strange happened at my house last night, John.

John: Really, Angela? What?

Angela: While my brother and I were watching TV, we heard someone at the front door. My brother went to answer it, but there was no-one there.

John: That is strange. Were you worried?

Angela: Not at first, but then it happened again a few minutes later.

John: What did you do?

Angela: Well, my brother said it was probably a joke. He thought it was one of his friends.

John: Hmm, that's not very funny.

Angela: No. But then, while I was standing in the kitchen, I saw something from the window. When I turned on the light, I saw a man! He was in our garden!

John: Oh, no! What did you do?

Angela: Well, our dog Sammie was in the garden too. When Sammie saw the man, he started to make terrible sounds. The man got scared and ran away.

John: That's really terrible. Who was that man?

Angela: I don't know. We told our parents about it when they got home from the cinema. They weren't happy about it, but at least no-one was hurt. I'm glad Sammie was there to help us!

John: Yeah, right! Good job, Sammie!

Unit 4 Listening

Tim: Hello?

Mum: Tim? Is that you?

Tim: Oh, hi, Mum. What's up?

Mum: I'm just calling to see how everything is going with the party.

Tim: Oh, everything's cool, Mum. I've already done everything! It's going to be great.

Mum: Really? Have you sent out the invitations yet?

Tim: The invitations? Of course I've sent them, Mum! I sent them last Tuesday by email, remember? I sent 50 invitations, to everybody!

Mum: And?

Tim: And what, Mum?

Mum: Well, the replies. Have you had any replies?

Tim: Yes, I've had lots of replies! So far I've had about 30 replies, but some people haven't answered yet ...

Mum: Thirteen? What? Only 13?

Tim: No, Mum. I said 30!

Mum: Oh, that's good. And what about the food? Have you ordered the food yet?

Tim: Yes, Mum, I have. Everything is...

Mum: Have you ordered sandwiches?

Tim: No, Mum, I haven't ordered sandwiches. I've ordered pizzas for the party. I've ordered 15 big pizzas for nine o'clock on Saturday night.

Mum: Nine? Isn't that too late? I mean, people will be hungry.

Tim: No, it's not late, Mum! Kids my age stay up later than you ... your friends are old.

Mum: What did you say? Did you call me 'old'?

Tim: No, Mum, just kidding! OK, Mum, I have to go.

Mum: No, wait, wait a minute. What about the decorations? Have you thought about that yet? What have you decided? How about flowers? Flowers are nice.

Tim: Mum, it's OK! We thought about little lights, but the party is outdoors and maybe we'll have a problem with the lights if it rains ... so we decided to use balloons. Everyone likes balloons.

Mum: Umm, yes. Nice idea ... OK. Good. Well done, you are organising everything very well. Now, the cake ... what about the cake?

Tim: Oh, Mum. The cake? Well ...

Unit 5 Listening

Woman: Good afternoon, Brighton Tourist Information. How can I help you?

Man: Hello. I'm thinking of visiting Brighton for a few days and I'd like some information about places to stay. I would like to stay somewhere near the centre.

Woman: OK. Let me see. There's the *Brighton Hotel*. That's at 21 Broad Street – that's B-R-O-A-D. It's in the centre.

Man: Do you know how much it costs for one night? I would like to pay around 50 pounds a night.

Woman: The rooms at the *Brighton Hotel* are 48 pounds per night for one person and 58 pounds per night for two persons.

Man: OK, great. Have you got the hotel's phone number?

Woman: Yes, it's 01273 840 322. You can phone them any time you like.

Man: Thank you. I'd also like some information on things to do in Brighton.

Woman: OK. Well, there's the art museum. And there's also the beach. Both places are very nice and the hotel is very close to them.

Man: Is the museum open every day?

Woman: The museum is open Tuesday to Sunday. It's closed on Mondays.

Man: Great. Thank you very much for your help.

Woman: Enjoy your stay in Brighton.

Man: Goodbye.

Woman: Goodbye.

Unit 6 Listening

Adam: Hey, Julia, how are you? Great to see you again! So, tell me about your new school. Is everything going well?

Julia: Yes, it is. I really like my school. I've met lots of new people and they're very friendly.

Adam: That's great! Do you live near your new school now? Can you walk to school?

Julia: Well no, unfortunately I can't! We live so far away and that's a problem for me. Mum can't drive me every day because she works, so I have to take a special school bus.

Adam: Why is that bad?

Julia: It's not really bad, but at the end of the day I'm really hungry and there's a rule about no food on the bus. Not even a little apple!

Adam: That's too bad! Hey, do you have to wear a uniform?

Julia: No, not every day. We must wear a uniform if we play sports with other schools but we don't wear it on school trips. Another rule is about mobile phones. You can take your mobile phone to school but you mustn't use your phone in the classroom. The teachers punish you for using it in the lesson!

Adam: Are your teachers nice?

Julia: Yes, but there is one new rule for me.

Adam: What do you mean?

Julia: Well, every time a teacher enters our classroom, we have to stand up. We mustn't stay in our chairs! But what I really like in my new school is Fridays!

Adam: Why? Can you go home early on that day?

Julia: No! On Fridays, we have lots of different clubs you can join. It's really good fun. I joined a video club. I'm going to make a music video!

Adam: Wow! That sounds so cool. We don't have clubs at our school. Lucky you!

Unit 7 Listening

Man: MP3 players are a very popular item these days. They're easy to use, very easy to carry, and they're used by both young people and adults. MP3 players are also quite new. The first MP3 player was created in 1997 by an American company called *Audio Highway*. The company named the music player *Listen Up* and it won many prizes for its exciting new design. Of course, this MP3 player couldn't hold the number of songs of today's MP3 players, and only 25 of these players were made. In 1998, a company in South Korea made their own MP3 player called *MPMan*. It was sold in the USA, but it wasn't very popular. Later that year, another American company called *Diamond Multimedia* created an MP3 player called the *Rio PMP300*. This player was sold with songs already on it, and it could play music for up to one hour. Although the *Rio PMP300* had a few problems, over 200,000 of these MP3 players were sold. Soon after, MP3 players became very popular and many players were made which could hold more songs and play music for longer.

Unit 8 Listening

Dialogue 1

Boy: Wow, this is amazing! Look at that flash of lightning! It reaches all the way from the sky to the ground. What a photo!

Girl: And look at the colour of the sky! It's red and orange! Fantastic! I wonder if the photographer was close to the lightning when he took it. I hope I can take a photograph like this one day!

Boy: No! It's really dangerous to be outside in a thunderstorm!

Dialogue 2

Girl: What's that weird sound?

Boy: What sound?

Girl: Can't you hear it? It never stops!

Boy: Hahaha! Now you sound weird! Those are the frogs! There's a big lake near our town. Frogs live there, they're very common in this area.

Girl: Frogs? Wow – I've never seen a real frog! I love frogs! We don't have frogs in the city where I live! Can we go and see them?

Dialogue 3

Grandfather: Peter, Peter? Is that you?

Peter: Oh, hi, Grandpa – yes it's me.

Grandfather: I've just heard the news on the radio. Is everyone all right?

Peter: Yes, Grandpa, we're all fine, but it was frightening. I was at school when it happened. When the ground started shaking, some of the younger children started crying. All the windows in our classroom broke and all our books fell on the floor.

Grandfather: Oh, dear!

Dialogue 4

Mum: Tim, I can't believe you're reading a book! You're usually playing video games! What a nice change!

Son: Mum, this book is so exciting! It's about a group of people who make films about thunderstorms. They've travelled all over the world to film thunderstorms.

Mum: Well, I'm very happy to see you so excited about a book, but isn't that dangerous? Have any of them been hit by lightning?

Son: Yes, twice! Cool, isn't it?

Mum: Umm, I'm not sure that I agree that it's cool, Tim, but enjoy the book!

Unit 9 Listening

Russell: Jane, do you think people eat a lot of food that's not healthy?

Jane: Yes, Russell, I do. You go to many places and you see people eating hamburgers, but not a lot where you see people eating fresh fruit or vegetables.

Russell: Well, I think people like fresh, healthy food. However, many places don't offer fresh food. They offer food that is made very fast and with a lot of oil. I think if places offered fresh food, more people would eat it.

Jane: I agree, but sometimes fresh food isn't healthy, you know.

Russell: What do you mean?

Jane: I went to a place that had salads the other day, and I got one. The salad had fresh vegetables in it, but it also had lots of oil. It wasn't healthy at all! I tried a little of it, but then I told the waiter I didn't want it because it had so much oil.

Russell: Ah, I see. So even salads aren't healthy!

Jane: Well, I've heard that many places have got small bottles of oil on the table so now I ask for a salad with no oil. Then, you can use the oil on the table to add how much you want.

Russell: That's a good idea! I'll try that next time I have a salad.

Unit 10 Listening

Julie: Fred, have you got a favourite person in your family?

Fred: Yes, I have. I love my own family of course, but I really like my cousin Angela.

Julie: How old is she?

Fred: She's 19. I think she's really nice.

Julie: What does she look like? Has she got long blonde hair like you?

Fred: No! She's got short dark hair. She's a very cheerful person. She's not pessimistic about anything!

Julie: She sounds really great! I'm looking forward to meeting her one day.

Fred: Her dad and my dad are brothers. They're very different! My dad is really tall and thin, but my uncle is short and he's got a huge moustache.

Julie: And has your uncle got a beard, too?

Fred: No, but he hasn't got any hair! He's a sociable, funny guy. And he's really artistic too, just like his daughter.

Julie: Really? What does she do?

Fred: Well, she wants to be a photographer, but at the moment she works in an office.

Julie: Is she very athletic?

Fred: Yes, she is. She enjoys sports and she loves cooking, but her favourite hobby is photography, of course. Look, this is one of her photos.

Julie: Wow! She's a really good photographer!

Unit 11 Listening

Karen: Hi, I would like to try on a dress, please.

Shop assistant: OK. I can help you with that. What dress did you have in mind?

Karen: I was thinking of buying a green dress. Do you have anything like that?

Shop assistant: Yes, take a look over here. These dresses are very comfortable and they come in three colours: blue, green and yellow. Here's a green one right here. What do you think?

Karen: It's very nice. Can I try it on?

Shop assistant: Sure. The dressing rooms are over there. ... So, did it fit OK?

Karen: No, I think I need a larger size.

Shop assistant: Hmm, OK. ... Well, I don't see a larger size in green. What about blue?

Karen: Yes, that seems OK.

Shop assistant: Would you like to try this one on to see if it fits?

Karen: Well, no. I think it will be OK. The other dress was just a little bit too small.

Shop assistant: OK. I'm sure that one will fit you better.

Karen: Thanks for you help.

Shop assistant: You're welcome!

Unit 12 Listening

Woman: *Get Fit Gym*, good morning, how may I help you?

Man: Oh, hello, yes, I'd like some information about your gym, please.

Woman: Certainly. Have you ever joined a gym before?

Man: Yes, but I'm new to this town. I've just moved here and I'd like to start working out again as soon as possible. May I come and see the gym?

Woman: Certainly. Our address is 290 – that's two nine o, Milton Road.

Man: Sorry? Did you say Miller Road?

Woman: No, Milton Road – M-I-L-T-O-N.

Man: Umm, I haven't got a car. Can I get there by bus?

Woman: Yes, easily. There are three different buses that stop right outside the gym, the number 9, number 14B and number 295.

Man: Great. Oh, and one last thing, could you tell me how much the gym is for one month?

Woman: Well, usually it costs 30 pounds for one month, but today we have a special price. If you join the gym today, you will only pay 15 pounds a month for the whole of next year.

Man: Really? You mean for the next 12 months I pay only 15 pounds a month?

Woman: Yes, that's right.

Man: That's amazing! Oh, I have one more question. Is there a swimming pool in the gym?

Woman: Yes, there are two swimming pools – a very large pool and a small pool for children under 12 years old. We also have an indoor basketball court and a tennis court.

Man: Really? I've always wanted to take up tennis! Do I have to pay more for tennis lessons?

Woman: Yes. For a one-hour lesson you have to pay five pounds.

Man: Finally, what are the opening hours of the gym?

Woman: The gym opens every day from 6am until 11pm including the tennis courts and the basketball court. The hours for the swimming pool are different, though. Some days of the week, the pool closes earlier than the gym.

Man: Oh, really? What days?

Woman: On Mondays and Thursdays, both swimming pools close at 6pm so that we can clean the pools. If you would like to call the pool office, the number is 0219 7345.

Man: Sorry, did you say 0219 7455?

Woman: No. 7-3-4-5.

Man: OK, got it! If I can leave work early today, I'll come this afternoon to see the gym. It sounds perfect, though. Thanks for your help.

Woman: You're welcome. We look forward to seeing you this afternoon – and don't forget the special cost for one year! Just 15 pounds a month!

Man: Don't worry, I won't forget! Bye.

Unit 13 Listening

Dialogue 1

Karen: How long will it take you to get here by bus, Mark?

Mark: Oh, I'm not coming by bus. I'm coming by train. It's faster.

Karen: Oh, I see. In that case, you should take a plane. That's the fastest.

Mark: Yes, but a plane is expensive.

Dialogue 2

Rebecca: When are you coming to my house tomorrow?

Stephen: Well, I'm leaving my house at 2.30. I think it will take me 30 minutes to get there, so probably around three.

Rebecca: Oh, good. Lisa will be here at 3.30. Then we can go shopping.

Dialogue 3

George: How long will you be in London?

Samantha: I'll be there from the 28th to the 30th April.

George: Oh, good! Will I get to see you?

Samantha: Of course! I haven't made plans on the 29th. I'll come by your house then.

Dialogue 4

Jenny: Where is the film showing? At Cinema 8?

Frank: No. It's at the cinema in Wesley Shopping Centre.

Jenny: OK. Do you want to meet a little early for coffee?

Frank: Sure. I know a great café near the shopping centre.

Jenny: Sounds good.

Unit 14 Listening

Welcome to *News of the Week*. And as all you listeners know, every week we tell you about three new websites that are our favourite sites! Well, this week we want to tell you about three sites that we've found and these are all news sites! So, are you ready?

The first site is a news site – but this site is about new video games! And here's the good news! This is a site where you can play new video games free! But sorry – the bad news is you can only play free for one hour – after 60 minutes you have to buy the game if you really like it! The new video game that we loved is called *Mystery Planet*. The site says *Mystery Planet* is perfect for children aged 14 or older, but we all had a great time playing ... so maybe it's fun for adults too!

The second site we discovered this week is also a news site, but this time it is news about animals. Yes, animals! This amazing site has news from all around the world about creatures on our planet. This week, the site was about animals from Africa! So, if you want to learn more about the beautiful animals from Africa, this is the news site for you!

The third news website, our favourite site this week, is not about video games or animals. This news site is all about sports news: skiing, football, skateboarding and even mountain climbing! This is a wonderful site where you can watch and read about all the sports news around the world! My favourite news video on this sports site this week was about mountain climbing. A team of 10 mountain climbers from different countries decided to make a film about climbing and you can watch this wonderful film on the site too. It's called *Climb to the Sky*! Unbelievable! So, if you think news is boring – you're wrong! Watch *Climb to the Sky* and you'll be amazed. I'm sure you'll love it!

So, there you are. Something for everyone. Three fantastic sites about video games, animals and sports news! Next week ...